# 50 Shades
# of
# Lipstick Leadership

50 Stories from
Empowering & Inspiring Women
Volume 1

Susanne Mueller, M.A.
Take it from the Ironwoman

# LOYALTY

"Have you ever wanted to travel to new places but found yourself limited by time and money? Dive into Susanne Mueller's book, filled with podcast conversations featuring women who have had extraordinary experiences. Their stories will take you to distant and nearby horizons without you needing to leave your seat. Plus, they might just inspire you to explore your journey and share your stories in the future." - Elena Ferrer, Ed.D., holds a Doctoral Degree in Health and Behavior Studies from Columbia University, New York, NY, and a Master's Degree in Psychology.

*******************

"This inspiring book is about incredible women who strive to achieve their dreams under the motto 'When you realize a dream is no longer a dream.' It's also about personal growth through continuous learning, being a good listener, and leader, and setting an example for others who need encouragement. Remember, you are solely responsible for creating your unique story: 'Be Bold, Brave & Brilliant.'" - Yvonne Lucrezia Condrau, Screenwriter

*****************

"Never give up—your greatest opportunity may be just around the corner! I've recently turned sixty, and I can honestly say it's the best stage of my life. Throughout my life, I dreamed of retiring early at 55, with the financial freedom to travel and empower Yucatecan women to become the leaders that the 21st century demands. I worked tirelessly towards this goal, and by 55, I had achieved everything I had longed for. However, the unexpected arrival of the pandemic shattered my plans and forced me back into the workforce. Now, five years later, I am returning to the path I had to leave behind, determined to create the space I envisioned for Yucatan women to grow and thrive. My lesson learned is that together, we can overcome any obstacles that stand in our way." - Janin Ricalde, Founder of Women Leadership and Beyond

************************

"'50 Shades of Lipstick Leadership' is a captivating collection of stories featuring confident, extraordinary girls and women who forge connections that transcend borders and time zones. It reminds us that every obstacle presents an opportunity for growth, and together, through shared experiences and collective wisdom, we can create a more compassionate and understanding world. These women's voices have a transformative impact, shaping our world towards a future enriched by those who dared to dream and persevered against all odds." - Sandra Ineichen, proud Mama of one of the Glitter Glam Girls

************************

"Susanne highlights and celebrates the resilience and power of each woman in her leadership journey, inspiring confidence and reshaping our understanding of success. She captures the essence of women's empowerment, encouraging them to lead authentically through the principles of Learning, Listening, and Leading!" - Destiny J. Cool, e-counselor for EDsnaps.

I sent a copy of my book "Lipstick Leadership – Empowering and Inspiring Women who dare to Lead" (2021) to Kamala Harris, the first female Vice President of the United States, and candidate to become the first female President of the United States. A few weeks later, I received this heartfelt appreciation from her. This serves as a reminder that each of us has the potential to make a significant impact!

P.S. I'll be sure to send her another copy of this book!

# LOVE

To my mother, Elsbeth Barben, who completed the pilgrimage to Santiago de Compostela, Spain.
*and*
To my sister, Professor Dr. Barbara Müller, who achieved a Black Belt (2nd Dan) in Karate.

# Contents

# LESSONS

## Lipstick Leadership Lessons

### Listening

Downloading, active listening, and hearing what has not been said.

### Learning
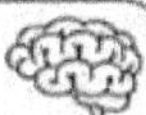

Lifelong learning is crucial for success; when we cease learning, our learning muscle weakens.

### Leading

Leadership is significant; everyone has the potential to lead and choose their path in life. Leading others requires utilizing all your talents.

### Lipstick Leadership

Lipstick is more than just cosmetics. In 2022, the beauty industry was valued at $430 billion and continues to grow globally. 

### Luxury Look

The Future is Feminine.

### Social Wellness

Connecting with wonderful people enhances overall happiness.

### Podcasting

This medium involves communication, active listening, and learning about others.

### Mental Fitness

A healthy mind, positive thoughts, and nutritious food are essential. Dream BIG, start now.

# LEAP

**Did you know?**

- In 2022, the **Beauty Industry generated around $430 billion.** This includes skincare, fragrance, makeup, haircare, and lipstick! "Beauty is now an industry that many people, from top-tier financiers to A-list celebrities, want to be part of." And it keeps growing every year worldwide.
- **"Take it from the Ironwoman" has 400+ podcast episodes in five languages and guests from all continents.**
- By publishing more than 21 episodes "Take it from the Ironwoman" is in the **World's Top 1% of Podcasters.**
- Making a 15-minute podcast episode can take about **5 hours.**

**It's about:**

- Finding the right guest, researching them, reaching out, booking, and then recording the episode—which is the **fun part.**
- Then comes the tech stuff: **editing, balancing the sound,** adding intros and music. This can be quite tedious for someone like me who isn't very tech-savvy!
- Once the podcast is ready, it's time to market it and share it on social media to get global exposure.

# LIFELONG LEARNING LETTERS

*"I never dreamed about success. I worked for it."*
– Estee Lauder, American businesswoman

Here, you can discover fifty inspiring and extraordinary stories of lifelong learners, featuring remarkable women from all walks of life. It could even include your story one day. Each narrative is unique, offering different perspectives and energies. Together, we share the goal of making the world a better place, one day at a time. Now, it's your turn to enjoy these stories from around the globe.

Most of these conversations took place during the 2020 pandemic. These inspiring, educational, and moving stories kept me going through the lockdown. It was all about building genuine relationships and forming a true community of learners and leaders by listening to their stories. This should be the beginning of building a global network for everyone. Stories are important for making the world a better place.

All these stories come from the podcast conversations on "Take it from the Ironwoman." Some guests have moved on since then, but when we spoke, it was a special moment. Let's support them all and celebrate their successes together. Onwards we go together: lifelong learning lessons for all!

This book features quotes **only** from remarkable female leaders across various industries. While we often use

inspirational quotes from men, it's important to recognize the power of female voices too. The idea of learning from others comes from the weekly blog I have been writing since 2010. What began as a travel blog has since evolved into a focus on learning and leadership.
(www.smuellernyc.blogspot.com)
How did it all start? In 2010, my job was being eliminated, and I needed some time to recuperate. Was that the start of burnout? I couldn't see myself jumping from one corporate job to another without a well-deserved break to heal and regroup in between.
So, I decided to volunteer my time in India. Around that time, Elizabeth Gilbert's book "Eat, Pray, Love" had just come out, and I started blogging. I thought to myself, if she can do it, so can I. Having worked in the airline industry for a long time, the travel bug had never left me. I packed my belongings, and at 4am in the morning, two gentlemen were waiting for me in Hyderabad, India, holding a sign that said "Ms. Mueller." How did I know it would work out and they would be there for me? I trust my intuition in life. I had a feeling it would work, and it did. That marked the beginning of a new chapter in my life, where I became more curious and embraced every opportunity and possibility that came my way.
Initially, I knew I couldn't adopt "Eat, Pray, Love" or Einstein's formula $E=mc^2$ as the cornerstone for my blog. Using such iconic phrases would be misleading – so I searched for my own formula for success. After contemplating for some time, $E=PL^3$ came to mind. E stands for good energy, healthy living, and positive thoughts; P represents play, where I explore important ideas and spark

innovative thoughts; and L³ symbolizes lifelong learning, which I consider essential – if you stop learning, you start to stagnate.

In the VIA character assessment (https://www.viacharacter.org/), my top characteristic is **"LIFELONG LEARNING."** From a young age, my mom noticed I slept surrounded by books – they've always been like invisible friends to me. Even now, when I visit friends, I'm drawn to their bookshelves. Once, I visited a house without books, which felt strange and empty – something crucial was missing. Books are a vital part of my life.
For years, I've challenged myself to read at least one book per month, sometimes more. While one book per month might not seem like much, I prefer setting achievable and realistic goals rather than overwhelming myself with a book per week. My weekly blog, which has continued beyond my time in India, is filled with valuable insights – each post is like exploring a bookstore with diverse sections catering to a broad, global audience.

Fast forward to today, I embarked on a new learning journey – podcasting. What I find most fulfilling about podcasting is the art of interviewing. To have a meaningful, engaging, and insightful conversation, I begin by researching the person to ensure they are a good fit for my podcast. However, I believe everyone has a unique story to share. For me, it's all about asking the right questions.

As an executive coach specializing in leadership, I've honed my questioning skills, and podcasting has further enhanced my ability to listen attentively. Initially, I outline a plan or idea for where the podcast conversation might lead. Yet, if intriguing aspects or experiences emerge during our 15-minute chat, I'm open to adjusting the plan. My goal is to learn about the person, and the conversation revolves around their story itself. It's about showcasing their experiences, insights, and what they bring to the table – it's never about me. This mirrors my approach in coaching sessions. I provide a safe space and guide the client, but I don't aim to solve all their problems; often, clients already possess the answers they seek. Sometimes, all that's needed is a moment of realization or reassurance.

Now is the opportune moment to harness the valuable lessons from lifelong learning and conversations, transforming them into a tangible piece like a book to be shared with others. The central theme will focus on lifelong learning, encompassing the principles of **learning, listening, and leading.**

*"Leadership at its core is about harnessing others' efforts to achieve something no one can achieve alone."*
- Amy C. Edmondson, Author and Professor of Leadership, Harvard Business School

All these remarkable women have faced and overcome significant obstacles, each encountering pivotal moments from which we can all glean valuable lessons. Moreover, the book will feature conversations with women from around the world. I always emphasize and embrace a global perspective

– it's crucial to me to highlight how different yet interconnected we all are, learning from diverse cultures.

During my time working with the airline, particularly in the Lost and Found Department at Zürich Airport, I had the privilege of interacting with people from myriad cultures. I vividly recall meeting a teacher from Madagascar, which was a unique opportunity afforded by my job. I made it a point to ask questions and listen attentively to their story. This reflects my unyielding curiosity and thirst for continuous learning. It's about enabling dreams to come true for everyone. If you can't travel to distant places, why not learn from locals through my podcast conversations or by reading this book?

It's always about taking one step at a time and approaching each day with intention. Every step should move us forward in the right direction. We rarely step backward; therefore, it's essential to focus on looking forward and progressing in the right direction.

*"If you want to go fast, go alone,*
*if you want to go far, go together."*
- African proverb

# Glitter Glam Girls

## A Success Story of Two Young Entrepreneurs

*"Give the children love, more love and still more love – and the common sense will come by itself."*
– Astrid Lindgren, author of Pippi Longstocking

"Glitter Glam Girls" is a story that serves as a wakeup call for many. Essentially, their inspiring story embodies all three elements of **learning, listening, and leading.**
Find your best friend in school, dream big, and start your venture. Even during the challenging times of the pandemic, it's possible to achieve something extraordinary. Perhaps, in some ways, difficult times are the right times to act. Do we ever truly have "easy times"? That's a question I often ponder when people mention "difficult times." Unfortunately, we tend to remember difficult times more readily than the good times – it's curious how this works. Ideally, we should remember the good times more vividly than the challenging ones.
The two girls remind me a bit of Pippi Longstocking – now is their time to impress the world in their own unique way. Remember the story? Pippi Longstocking lives alone with her horse and monkey in a large house. She's incredibly curious and always finds joy in doing fun, helpful things for others. Life with her is always an adventure.
Two young CEOs sharing their incredible journey: **The Glitter Glam Girls** – Ella and Naima (last names withheld for privacy) – were invited to be featured on the one

hundredth episode. Why? Because they are remarkable, forward-thinking CEOs who have made a significant impact. In March 2020, they launched their successful venture on the school playground during recess. Their goal was to earn money by creating crafts they both enjoy. Being best friends, they always think alike.

**Who picked the name?** Ella came up with the name while she was in the shower. She felt it suited both of their personalities well. Another name that crossed her mind was "Unicorn," but after discussing it with Naima, they settled on **"Glitter Glam Girls."** Naima explained that she didn't like the name "Unicorn" because it seemed too playful. They both agreed that "Glitter Glam Girls" was a more fitting and powerful way to describe themselves as girls.

At the young age of ten, they launched their own **website**. Initially, they received some assistance, but they quickly became proficient by learning the basics and soon became experts. They started by uploading pictures and even creating their own videos. Ella focused on decorations, while Naima worked on writing the descriptions.

Today, their offerings include a variety of holiday cards such as Halloween, Christmas, Valentine's Day, and Mother's Day cards. They take pride in custom-designed cards that they create on demand from their home.

**What did you learn when you first started?** We learned a lot about managing money, tracking orders, and updating our website.

**What are your Leadership Secrets?**

**Naima**: Our secret is knowing each other well and collaborating closely, which always leads to success.

**Ella:** Working together is enjoyable, and we support each other. Naima gives me advice frequently, and I do the same for her.

**Successes**: Today, I received a holiday package order from my aunt in London.

**Wisdom:** It's fulfilling to pursue something we both love with a good friend.

**Concerns**: As young and successful CEOs, balancing your business ventures with schoolwork can be challenging.

**Glitter Glam Girls:** We usually did our website after school when we finished all our work. That was mostly the moment when we both had time because later in the day, we either had lessons or after-school programs. Further, it wasn't that hard to combine schoolwork with our own business because we were all stuck at home anyway. We had tons of extra spare time. We were on FaceTime calls a lot, just making cards and adding more to the website.

Good luck to the young CEOs.

---

**Podcast Episode 100:** Glitter Glam Girls - Naima and Ella, 10-year-old CEOs on the 100th episode, October 15, 2020
**Contact Information:**
https://sites.google.com/view/glitter-glam-girls/home

# LEARNING

*"If you're sad, add more lipstick and attack."*
- Coco Chanel, French designer, businesswoman

The hunger for learning never stops, at least not for me. I always enjoyed going to school and discovering new things. While subjects like math, biology, and chemistry didn't always motivate me as much, I found my favorites in languages, geography, and humanities.

Later in life, when I returned to college, I challenged myself by taking classes in the sciences. It all started to make sense – why some concepts take years to fully grasp.

I believe the quality of the teacher is crucial. A teacher can either ignite passion or dampen interest in a subject. When a teacher is inspiring and serves as a role model, learning becomes significantly easier.

Initially, we learn to read, and then it shifts to reading to learn.

In the upcoming lessons on **learning,** we'll explore stories about education and leadership, as well as how education can intersect with business. Education is the cornerstone of both **learning and life itself.**

# Mimi Ugweje

## A World of Storytelling

*"Imagine how much happier you would be,*
*how much freer to be out true individual selves,*
*if we didn't have the weight of gender expectations."*
- Chimamanda Ngozi Adichie, award-winning Nigerian
American author


Mimi is a quiet yet resolute force behind several projects. She contributes to the EDsnaps E-Magazine, writes poetry, pursues learning opportunities, and supports the lipstick leadership initiative with enthusiasm.

Mimi - I currently live in the Bronx, New York, and I'm a college student majoring in English with a minor in journalism. I have a passion for storytelling, which I've enjoyed since middle school. Writing stories, poems, and creative pieces has always been a joy for me. Throughout middle and high school, English was my favorite subject because I loved writing essays and analyzing texts. In college, I've been immersed in rigorous learning, especially in dissecting and analyzing texts deeply. Last semester, I delved into critical theory, which taught me how to analyze texts through different critical lenses. I feel incredibly grateful and privileged to have had the opportunity to learn so much this semester.

**What is your dream?**

My dream is to write, to write every day. When I'm not writing, I want to read or spend time with people because stories are everywhere. In middle school, I used to watch love stories and try to recreate them by writing my own versions. I still have those old composition notebooks where I poured out my creative writing. Looking back now, some of those stories make me cringe because of the grammar mistakes and flawed characters. Despite that, I'm proud of myself for creating some good and enjoyable stories.

This dream persists, and I still aspire to become a writer, crafting books. Additionally, I'm drawn to journalism and even consider becoming an English professor at a college. There's time to explore all these paths.

**What do you do when you don't go to school?**

Outside of school, I tend to disconnect. I spend a lot of time listening to music and daydreaming. Being more of an introvert, I prefer staying in my room. It's during these quiet moments, with music playing, that ideas for writing often come to me.

---

**Podcast Episode 410:** Mimi – A College Professor in the Making, March 11, 2024

**Contact Information:** www.edsnaps.org

# Katie Watt

## Finding Grace Through Everyday Challenges

*"Let us make our future now and let us make our
dreams tomorrow's reality."*
– Malala Yousafzai, Pakistani female education
activist & Nobel Peace winner

If you ever need to collaborate with someone reliable, interesting, forward-thinking, and fun, Katie is your go-to person. I can personally vouch for her excellence. We've worked closely together on several highly successful and enjoyable business leadership projects, both online and in person.

**What hashtags do you use?**
Katie - I earned a Master's Degree in International Development from the University of Pittsburgh. I currently live in Salta, Argentina, with my husband and two kids. After working at a business school, I started my own business teaching English to academics and business professionals. I soon realized I could offer more than just teaching. My business is called **English Consulting Services.**

**How did you end up in Argentina?**
I come from a family of doctors and scientists, but I was more interested in history. I took many history classes, especially in Latin American history. I spent a summer in

Ecuador, some time in Chile, and then, of course, Argentina. At the end of my time at Ohio State, I applied for a Fulbright Scholarship to Argentina—and I won. At first, I was shocked, but then I became excited. I was thrilled to spend almost a year in Argentina as an English Teaching Assistant. I was assigned to Salta, where I met my husband.

**How would you describe that journey of a year?**
A year feels long when you're abroad by yourself, but you learn a lot about yourself. I read countless books when I was alone. At first, I had no friends, so it was a great time for deep self-reflection. Gradually, I started to come out of my shell, made friends, and began to really integrate into the local culture.

At the beginning of my year abroad, social media was just starting to take off. Skype was one of the only ways I could communicate with my family and friends back home. In a way, this forced me to reflect on who I wanted to be in this new place where nobody knew me. The town I lived in had just gotten its first ATM, and there was no internet in town. The nearest internet café was an hour away, and I used calling cards to stay in touch with my family and friends.

**Real tips for a successful year abroad:**
- Force yourself to be more outgoing, even if you're not naturally extroverted.
- Don't give up. I was homesick and wanted to go home. I cried a lot, but I kept going.
- Embrace the lonely moments; they will make you stronger.

- Journal your reflections about what you learn from the new culture and about yourself.
- Explore your new surroundings by going to the grocery store, walking around, seeing new blocks, and going down new streets. These small steps help you appreciate your new environment.
- Be patient—it takes time, but don't give up!

**Culture shock:**

I've been living in Salta for quite some time, but I still experience moments of culture shock. I get frustrated when things don't work the way I expect them to. Simple tasks, like going to the post office, can be a challenge. However, these experiences broaden your perspective, make you more patient with yourself, and help you appreciate the people around you. We all have our moments, but I've learned to speak from the heart.

---

**Podcast Episode 18:** Katie Watt – From the USA to Salta, Argentina, February 3, 2020
**Contact Information:** Instagram: @Katie Watt English

# Amanda Hsiung Blodgett | "Miss Panda"

## Embracing Connections across Borders

*"Optimism is the faith that leads to achievement."*
- Helen Keller, American author, disability rights advocate, political activist, lecturer

Let's be open and learn something from Amanda, aka Miss Panda. She is a Mandarin Chinese instructor, intercultural language consultant, podcaster, and author. We met virtually in the podcasting world in 2019.

**How can we encourage someone to learn a new language?**
Amanda - I have a podcast called **"Playful Chinese."** My approach is to have fun, which helps you relax while learning. Learning a new language isn't difficult; it's different. If you believe it's possible, you'll likely want to learn more. We focus a lot on listening: hearing something and then saying it out loud.

"Have you eaten?" is a very common greeting in Chinese. People are very concerned about whether you've had lunch, breakfast, or dinner. Food is important in Chinese culture; it's a way to check in and see how you're doing.

During our podcast episode, I learned how to say, "I love chocolate."

This is an important phrase for me: 我爱巧克力 (Wǒ ài qiǎokèlì).

**Let's learn from living abroad in diverse cultures:**
When I moved to **Morocco,** I was fascinated by its differences, especially the languages—French and Arabic. The further south you traveled, the more Arabic was spoken. Whenever I live in a different culture, I make sure to respect it. While in Morocco, I wore long pants and long-sleeve shirts, even in the warm weather, to show my respect for the host country. This effort to respect local customs is where building relationships begins. Making an effort to connect helps bridge cultural gaps.

When I lived in **Ecuador,** I saw the many cultures of South America and noticed their strong family bonds. For Mother's Day, flowers were everywhere. While we also see flowers in the United States and other places around the world, the way Ecuadorians celebrate Mother's Day highlights the deep importance of mothers in their lives.

When we moved in, my neighbor saw the truck with our belongings and immediately came to knock on my door to welcome me to the neighborhood. At that time, my Spanish was extremely limited, but we communicated through gestures and body language. I quickly understood that she was inviting me to her house for coffee and cake. Coffee is a simple word that is easily understood.

My children were concerned: "Mom, you don't really speak Spanish?" "Yes, I know, but let's try, why not?" It was a heartfelt but intense hour of coffee, exhausting my limited Spanish language skills. I had a headache afterward, but I felt that I had built a wonderful relationship and bridged the cultural gap once again.

**Wisdom:**
Always be open and ready for coffee with your neighbors. I enjoy sharing my meaningful and heartfelt experiences from living overseas. This is how I build relationships with those around me. People are kind and generous, reaching out to connect with outsiders and foreigners in their own countries. Make a point to learn something new each year. Anything is possible.

Thank you, mille merci, gracias, Xièxiè. (Thank you in Chinese)

**Happy moments:**
We had the chance to meet in Washington, DC. It's always a highlight for me to meet my podcast guests in person.

---

**Podcast Episode 170:** Amanda Hsiung-Blodgett - Learn Mandarin with Miss Panda, March 22, 2021
**Contact Information:** https://www.misspandachinese.com/

# Anette Carlisle

## A Mission for Female Leadership

*"Until we get equality in education,
we won't have an equal society."*
- Sonia Sotomayor, US Supreme Court Associate Justice

Anette - I live in Amarillo, Texas, I'm a research scientist, an evolutionary biologist, and an education advocate. I researched bats in graduate school. My journey led me here because my husband is an infectious disease doctor, and I grew up nearby. While raising our three boys over the past 30+ years, I've been deeply involved as a stay-at-home mom and community volunteer. My interest in education was sparked when my children started in public schools. I dedicated 19 years to the school board and am currently serving my 10th year on the Board of Regents at Amarillo College, where I recently chaired from 2022 - 2024. During this time, Amarillo College earned recognition as the top college in the nation by the Aspen Institute. I've also been active in nonprofit work, focusing on systemic change in education to lift people out of poverty and create better opportunities for all.

I'm also actively involved in **Leadership Women,** an organization with a 30+ year history that originated in Texas under a different name before becoming Leadership Women. Our primary focus is on two programs: Leadership Texas and Leadership America. Through these programs, we cultivate and empower women leaders by bringing together large groups of women from across the country and state.

In today's world, the need for strong women leaders is more critical than ever. It's our moment to step up. If not now, then when? We must increase the presence of strong women in leadership roles.

**Education, not poverty!** Education and combating poverty through education are significant, interconnected issues. How can we enhance education opportunities for everyone? I founded an organization called Panhandle 2020 (https://www.panhandle2020.org/) to unite different institutions and leaders around a shared agenda. This approach, now known as **collective impact,** aims to break down silos that often exist between sectors like K-12 schools, community colleges, four-year universities, and early childhood education.

Twenty years ago, we didn't have the term "collective impact," but our mission was to bring these entities together to understand and address each other's challenges. Today, we've established systems of support and integration. We collaborate on committees and cross-pollinate our boards, fostering a more cohesive approach to education and poverty alleviation in our communities.

I'm someone who relies on data. When you look at the numbers, 70% of our kids are on free and reduced lunch. When I first joined the school board 25 years ago, that figure was around 50%. This stark reality has been a driving force behind my work and the inspiration for my podcast, **"Anette on Education... and Maybe a Few Other Things."**

**Our podcast journey:** Susanne and I crossed paths in 2019 during a Podcasting Fellowship. I enrolled out of curiosity, uncertain if I would launch a podcast. My goal was to gather insights on how podcasting could align with our efforts in education and poverty reduction. It evolved into **"Anette on Education,"** a platform to share our work and insights.

For Mother's Day and Father's Day episodes, I came up with a fun concept that turned out to be a hit. On the Mother's Day episode, I interviewed my three sons, who were scattered across California and Kansas at the time. For Father's Day, I had the boys interview their dad. Previously, I had my husband, who is an expert in infectious diseases, on another podcast discussing the history of pandemics, which has become one of my most popular episodes to date.

**Susanne:** One of my all-time favorites is when Anette interviewed her neighbor, Jerome the Gnome. They discussed magical creatures, "gnoming" (coding), and the importance of getting along with others. Anette truly appreciated Jerome's presence on her podcast, bringing a touch of magic to the world.

---

**Podcast Episode 60:** Anette Carlisle - Anette on Education - Amarillo, Texas, July 8, 2020
**Contact Information:**
https://www.anettecarlisle.com/about-anette

# Oluremi Hamid

**Female Resilience in Engineering and Tech**

*"Be unreasonable, strong-headed, and stubborn about
eliminating any obstacle that stands in your way."*
- Bilikiss Adebiyi-Abiola, CEO, Wecyclers


My name is Oluremi (Adiat) Hamid, though my full name is Oluwaremilekun, which means God has wiped my tears. I studied electrical engineering and currently live in Lagos, Nigeria, where I am married and work. My focus is on renewable energy, specifically providing solar solutions for homes and small to medium-sized businesses. I am passionate about advocating for clean energy.

We connected through the **Cherie Blair Foundation for Women,** a mentorship program supporting women entrepreneurs in growing their businesses. Women often face challenges as minorities in many aspects of life. However, women are also mothers and creators of life. Investing in a woman means more than supporting one individual—it means investing in an entire community. Women contribute significantly to their families and communities, creating a ripple effect of positive impact.

**How did you get into the STEM field?**
Well, back in secondary school, I wasn't initially interested in math and was just an average student. It wasn't until my second year that I started to develop a real interest in math

and physics. Balancing my studies with my passion for basketball was crucial. I would play basketball in the morning and then focus on my studies after school. I dedicated four hours every day to practicing math because I knew that consistent effort was the key to improvement—whether in math or sports!

In 2017, I founded an initiative called "Inspired for STEM." As a STEM trainer, I feel privileged to have pursued engineering, a path that wasn't commonly chosen by females in the past. Today, more women are studying science, technology, engineering and math, yet they often do not pursue careers in these fields. We are working to change that narrative and encourage more females to consider careers in STEM.

**Let's talk business:**
The name of my company is **Hydren Energy Limited.** We specialize in renewable energy, offering solar solutions tailored for homes, mini, and micro-businesses across Nigeria. Our aim is to become the top choice renewable energy provider for our target customers in Nigeria.

We provide solar solutions that ensure homes and businesses can power office equipment or household appliances for at least twelve hours daily. Our goal is to provide uninterrupted electricity from morning until the next day, utilizing the abundant and free solar energy available in Nigeria. Looking ahead, we are seeking investors who share our vision and believe in the potential of our business.

**Ingredients for success involve a combination of several factors:**

- **Resilience and Standing Your Ground:** Especially as a woman in engineering and technology, resilience is key in a male-dominated industry.
- **Belief in Yourself:** Have the mindset of proving yourself, saying "I am going to show you that I am better than you."
- **Follow Your Own Dream:** Pursue your own dreams, not someone else's. Your dreams are uniquely yours.
- **Belief in the Achievability of Your Goals**: Whatever you want to achieve is possible. Don't let anyone undermine your ambitions.
- **Consistency:** Stay committed despite challenges. Giving up is never an option.
- **Understanding the Value of Effort:** Nothing in life is truly free. If something seems free, someone else has invested in it.

These principles form the foundation for achieving success in any field or endeavor.

**What is happening in Lagos over the weekend?**
In Lagos, weekends are filled with lively celebrations and gatherings. Nigerians have a deep love for enjoying life, especially through parties. Almost every Saturday, you can expect at least one event—whether it's a wedding reception, a celebration of a new baby, or a traditional naming ceremony.

These gatherings are marked by music, dancing, and a variety of delicious foods. Saturdays in Lagos are synonymous with fun and festivity, emphasizing our strong sense of family where even cousins are considered as close as sisters.

As Oluremi puts it, "We only have one life," reminding us to embrace every opportunity for joy and connection with loved ones.

---

**Fast forward:** She is pursuing another Master's Degree in Manufacturing Engineering Technology at Western Illinois University in Macomb, IL, to advance her education.

---

**Podcast Episode 31:** Oluremi Hamid – The STEM Expert from Lagos, Nigeria, April 6, 2020
**Contact Information:** Instagram: @Hydren Energy

## Journeying through Self-Discovery

*"I don't go by the rule book.*
*I lead from the heart, not the head."*
- Princess Diana of Wales

Isil - originally from Turkey and now residing in Munich, Germany, shares many similarities with me. Both of us have relocated from one country to another and share passions as coaches, podcasters, and writers. Her book titled *"The Gift of Being Unfulfilled at Work* – A Journey to self-discovery and life energy" invites you to embark on a transformative journey of self-discovery and reclaiming your life energy.

**What are the hashtags that describe you well?** Unique, human experience, moving, love, coaching, community, life in general, fun, dance, being together.

**Let's dance together:** It all began when I visited Munich with a group from my university in Turkey, primarily to experience Oktoberfest. At the airport, we struggled to figure out how to buy tickets to the city center from the machine. It felt like hours passed before someone tapped me on the shoulder and handed me a ticket, saying, "Welcome to Munich." That moment sparked something within me. Throughout my trip, I encountered countless acts of kindness and welcoming gestures that made me fall in love with the city. Life presented me with an opportunity to move, and I seized it. Soon after, I relocated to Munich and began working in a financial institution. However, after a few years, I realized I had lost touch with what truly fulfilled me—working closely with people. I felt disconnected and numb. Despite the challenges, I viewed this period positively as it prompted deep reflection:

- What could I do next?
- What would bring me fulfillment?
- What skills and qualities do I possess?
- What values are important to me?
- How can I align my passions with earning a living?

I embarked on my coaching journey by enrolling in a coaching certification program, reigniting my true passion. Embracing the principle that you become the **average of the five people** you spend the most time with, I initially attended meetups where fellow coaches openly shared their experiences. I found these gatherings intimate and supportive, fostering a deep learning environment about coaching. It was at one of these meetups that I met Elena, who would later become my co-founder at the academy. Together, we began organizing workshops and gatherings for individuals interested in coaching. Responding to the needs expressed by prospective students, we established **"BeCoach Academy."** Our approach started with a simple questionnaire and short interviews to understand what was important and needed. We discovered that many people were eager to either become coaches themselves or gain deeper self-awareness.

Today, our academy attracts students from diverse age groups and backgrounds. While our primary language of instruction is English, we also accommodate German-speaking students.

**Who is your ideal client? Who energizes you?** I enjoy the creative journey—beginning in one place and ending up somewhere entirely new. Coaching for me is about staying present in the moment, similar to **dancing in the moment.** I find it hard to categorize or confine these individuals. What matters is being open, energized, brave, and able to express emotions without fear of judgment. My clients are vibrant - they thrive on exploring new experiences and cultures, and they are passionate about enjoying life to the fullest.

**Coachable moment:** It seems that what you've described as your ideal client reflects characteristics that resonate with who you are personally - being open to new cultures and embracing creativity.

**Isil:** Thank you for pointing that out. I hadn't realized it, but I suppose I've been envisioning my ideal client as someone similar to myself.

---

**Podcast Episode 10:** Isil Uysal - Integration in Munich, Germany, December 9, 2019
**Contact Information:** https://www.becoach-academy.com/

# Libby Romfh

## Change Plus Management

*"Who knows what women can be when they are
finally free to be themselves."*
- Betty Friedan, American writer, and activist

Libby and I first met at the monthly meetings of the Organizational Development Network in New York. These gatherings provided not only opportunities to exchange ideas and network but also to discuss life, which eventually led to us becoming friends.

*"Libby received her first rejection letter from Random
House at the age of five, which she truly deserved."*

**What is the name of your blog:**
The name of my blog is **Change + Management**. I began it in 2017, and it has transformed over time. During the pandemic, I shifted to focus more on personal growth for both myself and those around me. As of 2024, I'm challenging myself to write daily about books. Recently, my incredibly thoughtful husband downloaded an app and scanned and uploaded every single book from my collection. I now have approximately 4,500 books to explore and share on my blog.

**What are the criteria for your books? What are you most drawn to?**

I have an omnivorous appetite for books, likely stemming from my years working in the book industry where I was constantly surrounded by them. My collection includes books on unusual topics, such as dirt, the molasses flood in Boston, or something local I found while visiting a bookstore. I've always been drawn to odd books that nobody else seemed to want.

I read a wide variety of genres: mystery, science fiction, nonfiction, horror, romance, and even children's books to reconnect with my inner child. Due to my professional interests, I also have many books on coaching, business, and management. I must have a whole shelf and a half dedicated to figuring out what you want to be when you grow up. Additionally, I have books about travel, animals, nature, and the diversity of life. In short, I love books that transport me to another world, whether it's a historical setting or a fictional universe.

I'm blogging daily about a book, but I'm also sharing what the book means to me and what's on my mind. My blog is a reflection of myself, my life, and my perspective on the world. It's my way of sharing insights and connecting with others.

**What is your writing routine for blogging?**

A few years ago, I read a book on change management that discussed the **transformative power of writing.** In one example, four thousand middle managers were affected by a factory closure. They were divided into two groups for an experiment. Both groups received outplacement services, including support groups, resume assistance, and help finding new jobs. However, only the second group was assigned to write for 20 minutes each day on any topic they chose, without having to share what they wrote.

Interestingly, the group that wrote daily found new employment at a statistically higher and faster rate than the group that didn't write. This inspired me to commit to writing for 20 minutes each day, whether for my blog, in my diary, or working on fiction or nonfiction projects.

**What do you do when you're not working (aka blogging)?**
I'm a walker. Walking stimulates my brain and boosts my creativity. I've had weekends where I walked ten miles on both Saturday and Sunday. In New York, I'd wander through Central Park, letting my thoughts flow freely. Sometimes, an idea would strike, and I'd sit on a bench, pull out my notebook, and jot it down before continuing my walk. The process often repeats, with new ideas emerging as I keep walking. This blend of physical activity and mental creativity is incredibly refreshing for me.

---

**Podcast Episode 418:** Libby Romfh – 365 Books, Daily Blogger, April 15, 2024
**Contact Information:**
https://changeplusmanagement.blog/category/change/

Sheila Harkatz

## Mastering Finance and Independence

*"People respond well to those that are sure of what they want."*
- Anna Wintour, Editor-in-Chief, Vogue

Sheila and I met when she mentored me for one of the first online classes I taught, "Game Changing Leadership." This was before Zoom classes became popular, so I needed some guidance. I've learned a lot from Sheila—she is a fantastic, caring, creative, and fun woman with a forward-thinking mindset. Above all, she has an abundance of energy to share with others.

Sheila - I was born in Argentina but I am also American. I lived in the U.S. for over 13 years and have now returned to my hometown of Buenos Aires. Upon moving back, I founded a community of women called **"Mujeres en Carrera"** (Women in Careers). This initiative focuses on strengthening women's economic autonomy, personal finance skills, and STEM employability.

Mujeres en Carrera is an Edtech initiative aimed at promoting the inclusion of women and girls in finance and business to reduce poverty and vulnerability among women. Our objective is to empower women by teaching them about finance, enabling them to speak the language of business, negotiate effectively, become financially independent, and make powerful decisions for themselves. These skills are crucial for both personal and professional life.

We offer an online community with free educational resources, primarily targeting women, but we welcome people from different communities. There is a specific need for women to become financially literate, and we all need to work together to achieve this. We support all 17 United Nations Sustainable Development Goals.

**What was the eye-opening moment for you?**
I arrived in Argentina in October 2018 after living in Mexico for some time. As I was settling in with my family and preparing to look for a job, I noticed a significant disparity in workplace opportunities for men and women. Despite my international background and experience, when I applied for jobs at big companies, the focus wasn't on my skills, global work experience, or industry knowledge. Instead, I was questioned about my age, marital status, children, and whether I had someone to care for them while I was at work.

I was stunned by these questions. I fully understand the demands of hard work, having worked extensively in the United States, and I'm not afraid of challenges. Unfortunately, I didn't land the corporate job I wanted. This experience opened my eyes to the persistent gender biases in the workplace and inspired me to take action.

After these awful experiences, I realized I needed to learn something new to enhance my resume. Things started to change when I began studying coding and participated in a

FinTech Hackathon organized by Media Chicas, an NGO dedicated to recruiting girls and women into STEM careers and banking. This experience gave me the extra push to start my own initiative.

I created my own website, produced videos, and posted on Instagram. I built a free community for interested subscribers. Thanks to my hard work, several companies invited me to speak about the importance of financial literacy and bridging the gender gap in finance. This journey allowed me to turn a negative experience into a positive opportunity to empower others.

**Challenging the Status Quo:**
I am aware that very few people can invest online because it requires a bank account, and sadly, not everyone in the Hispanic world has access to one. However, the most important thing is to show every young woman what it means to invest in herself and her future. The tech aspect is one side, but there is a significant mental mindset shift that must be addressed and changed.

Historically, women have often been the heads of households, responsible for taking care of children, cooking, and doing the laundry. In some countries, there may be some help, but when it comes to financial decisions, it is still often the man who makes the final call. Now is the time to educate women in financial literacy.

I believe in going the extra mile and addressing the root issues. Always surround yourself with diverse people from various backgrounds, and never give up.

Good luck. Mucha suerte. Nos vemos. Gracias.

---

**Podcast Episode 168:** Sheila Harkatz – Mujeres en Carrera – Women Financial Literacy, March 17, 2021
**Contact Information:**
https://www.mujeresencarrera.com.ar/

# Kate Edwards

**Creativity & Innovation in the Restaurant Industry**

*"To me, leadership is not about being the loudest in the room."*
- Dame Jacina Ardern, former New Zealand prime minister


Thankfully, you helped guide me when I chose my coaching program. I'll always think of you when I think of coaching. We met in running classes in Central Park in New York. Runners always support each other; it's about building a lifelong support system.

Kate - I work as a consultant, author, executive coach, and educator in the hospitality industry, specializing in customer service, customer experience, and leadership. My journey began over 30 years ago in restaurants, where I started working while in college. What began as a means to earn money turned into a career path I hadn't anticipated. (https://kateedwardscompany.com)

Before transitioning to consulting in 2007, I spent several years gaining experience and climbing the ranks in various roles within restaurants. Notably, I spent seven years at Balthazar in New York, starting as a cocktail waitress and eventually becoming a manager and maître d'. During this time, I was also pursuing my passion for music on weekends, but I eventually realized I needed to focus on one path to achieve my career goals effectively.

I made a list of advantages and disadvantages to help me decide, and ultimately chose to fully commit to the restaurant industry. I secured a position at Per Se in New York, a prestigious and sought-after restaurant at the time. My time there was pivotal in shaping my career path. After two years, I transitioned into consulting, specializing in assisting restaurant owners in realizing their vision through exceptional guest service.

**Are you Gordon Ramsey or Anthony Bourdain of the restaurant industry?**

Oh no! That's not me at all — I'm here to help. I don't yell at anyone. We really admire Anthony Bourdain for showing the real side of restaurant life. It's not all glitz and glamour; it's about tough, daily grind. Some might find it daunting, but there's beauty in it. Each day starts fresh with clean dishes and counters. We prep ingredients, cook delicious meals, welcome guests, serve them, and tidy up at the end of the night. There's a satisfying rhythm and energy in this routine — it's straightforward and consistent, day after day.

**What happened during the pandemic?**

During the pandemic, it was a shocking time for all of us in the industry. Many places closed down, which was frightening and disheartening. I reached out to everyone I knew, but the response was minimal. It became clear that people were deeply affected—emotionally and financially—by the prolonged shutdowns. Some did their best to honorably keep going, paying suppliers, staff, and rent despite the challenges. It was incredibly tough. I was afraid and wondered if my own business, focused on this industry, would ever recover.

**And then?**
It's been inspiring to witness how many brands swiftly adapted and thrived during this period. Many owners closed some locations or transformed their restaurants into production kitchens, focusing entirely on pickup and delivery.
With takeout, all you really need is space to set up a streamlined system for orders, pack everything neatly, and ensure it's all organized and ready to go. Normally, pickup and delivery are a smaller part of the business due to space limitations. However, during the pandemic, it became crucial for staying operational and surviving. I've seen some incredibly innovative approaches during those challenging times.

These changes have been both surprising and exciting. I've always believed that in this industry, creativity and innovation are key to keeping your brand alive. It's essential to observe what works, adapt quickly, evolve, and not wait for the competition to make the first move. This is the time to do something extraordinary.

Bon Appétit!

---

**Podcast Episode 166:** Kate Edwards - Look behind the Scenes of Hospitality, March 15, 2021
**Contact Information:** https://kateedwardscompany.com/

Joanna Perchaluk

## Running with Polar Bears

*"You do not travel if you are afraid of the unknown.
You travel for the unknown, that reveals you in yourself."*
– Ella Maillart, Swiss adventurer, travel writer,
photographer (1903 - 1997)


As a podcaster and coach, I always aim to disrupt and innovate. Why? Because if I have an idea for an interview guest, I go for it – that's my marathon mindset. I don't take NO for an answer. It was an honor to hear Joanna's life lessons. She's originally from Poland and claims she doesn't speak English, which isn't true. I met her through a Facebook group for women in sports, though the group is unfortunately no longer active.

She asked if the members could send her videos of our workouts from our locations to motivate her while she was at the Polish Polar Station in Spitzbergen, in the Arctic Circle. Thanks to technology, anything is possible.

My name is Joanna Perchaluk. I'm a meteorologist and the leader of the 42nd Polish Polar Expedition in Spitzbergen, in the Arctic Circle.

**What brings you to the Polar Station?**
I've been stationed here three times already. Initially, I was curious and wanted to experience something new and

different. The second time, I wanted to do everything I missed the first time. Now, this is my third time.

**Marathon races?**
The most memorable marathon race was my first one because I didn't know what I was doing. When I crossed the finish line, I said, "Let's do it again." Now, I know more about what I'm capable of and I'm ready to do it again.

**How did you get into this sport?**
Sports have always been a part of my life, from swimming and skiing to running. I'm a ski instructor in the winter and a sailing instructor in the summer. I was talking to my sister about how great it is that people are starting to run. I knew running a five-kilometer distance would be easy for me, so I did it. Then I learned about triathlon races, which are different because they require training in three disciplines: swimming, biking, and running. One day, while sipping my morning coffee, I found a race and signed up. I wanted to see how hard it would be. Later, I realized it wasn't the smartest idea since the ski season ended in March, leaving me only six weeks to prepare. But I did it. When you sign up, you go and do your best.

**And where do you train? What does your training ground look like?**
Currently, I'm in the Arctic, stationed here for eight months out of the year. Because of the low temperatures and the presence of polar bears and other animals, I do most of my training indoors. When the weather is good, I sometimes run outside, but I always have armed bodyguards with me to

watch for any danger. They alert me if there's any imminent threat. It's an adventure!

**What other hobbies do you have while living in the Arctic and training for triathlon races?**
Photography holds a special place in my life, and I love sharing my Arctic photos on Facebook and Instagram. I also enjoy water sports, sailing, diving, skiing, dog trekking, and crocheting during the long winter nights.

Thank you for sharing a glimpse into your exciting life and your photography.

**Fast forward:**
She spent four years at the polar station, serving as either the expedition leader or a meteorologist. Currently, she works as a circular economy and service manager at Decathlon Campus Polska. In 2023, she visited my home country, Switzerland, by bike.

---

**Podcast Episode 36:** Joanna Perchaluk – from the Artic - Working from Home, April 15, 2020
**Contact Information:** Instagram / Facebook: @Joanna Perchaluk

# Snezana Radojicic

## Cycling around the World

*"Nothing is impossible, the word itself says 'I'm possible."*
- Audrey Hepburn, actress and activist

Today is November 10, and while waiting for her to record her story for the podcast, I found out that we share the same birthday. I actually found her on Instagram while looking for adventurous women, and she really is one. When we spoke, she was in Bogota, Colombia, fixing her bike for her next adventure. Fixing a bike in South America can take a bit longer. I was happily browsing through her fabulous and entertaining Instagram, admiring her amazing journey. Let's celebrate our birthdays together, always! Happy Birthday!

Snezana - I am a teacher of literature, writer, and adventurer. Originally, I worked in an insurance company because I couldn't support myself as a teacher in Serbia. That feels like another galaxy now. Since I was a child, my dream was to live freely in the mountains, in a wooden house surrounded by nature, where I could write my books. I envisioned only visiting big cities to meet readers and share my adventures. I enjoy being an outsider, not part of the system. Since 2011, I've been on the road with my bike as a nomad, hence **"Ciklonomad."**

56

**How did it all start?**
When I first got into biking, I was searching for someone to join me, despite having no experience with bike travel. My initial plan was to travel with a few like-minded people for at least two years. I began with my then-boyfriend, who was from the United States. We connected through "Crazy Guy on the Bike," the largest portal for Bicycle Touring, which has a section for finding cycling companions. One thing led to another, and he visited me in Belgrade. We did a trial tour to Italy for a month, and during that time, we fell in love.

Afterwards, we embarked on a journey from Slovakia to Greece and Turkey. Along the way, we encountered numerous challenges stemming from our limited knowledge of each other. It wasn't easy spending entire days biking together, then sharing a tent with significant language barriers and cultural differences. Eventually, we broke up. Despite friends advising me to return home, citing concerns about being a woman alone in a Muslim country, I was determined not to give up on my dreams.

I kept going, even though I only had a budget of six euros per day back then. Don't ask me how I survived. On top of everything, I faced bicycle problems that couldn't be fixed. Yet, despite it all, I felt a profound happiness I'd never experienced before in my life. It made me realize: if this makes you so happy, why not keep going until it no longer serves you? ...and the rest is history.

For the first three and a half years, I cycled continuously. Sometimes I'd stay in one country longer to ease visa requirements, using the time to write a new book. I might stay six or seven months, simply enjoying the freedom to do as I pleased, entirely on my own terms.

**How to survive:** I rented out my apartment in Belgrade to finance my journey. In the beginning, there were times when I didn't have enough to eat, but surprisingly, I never felt hungry. I couldn't afford accommodation, so I relied on couchsurfing for a warm shower now and then. Finding reliable Wi-Fi was a challenge, and I couldn't afford hotel rooms. I'd spend hours in cafés, using their Wi-Fi to write my travel blog. I didn't have solar panels back then, so sometimes I'd ask people in hotels if I could use their Wi-Fi. I still don't have sponsors, but I run a blog where people can donate one Euro per month or more to read my posts.

**What do you pack for your adventures?**
Packing light for my travels has always been a challenge. In South America, it's especially tricky because of the diverse landscapes—coastlines, mountains, and the Amazon—all requiring different equipment for various seasons. I carry six bags on my bike: two in the front, two in the back, one in the middle, and one on the handlebar. The front bags are my "kitchen" where I store food. Depending on where I am, I either eat at local eateries or cook for myself. In tiny villages or deserts, I have to carry all my food and water.

I always pack at least one sleeping bag, a mat, and a tent. Another bag holds my clothes, electronics, and personal items. Typically, my gear weighs between 35 and 45 kilograms, depending on the season and how much food I need to carry. Despite the weight, I'm happy to have everything I need for my adventures.

**What's next?** I honestly don't know. I've never been one for planning.

**Happy moments:** I had the opportunity to meet her—she has such an adventurous spirit and prefers not to stay in one place for too long! Safe travels until we cross paths again somewhere around the world.

---

**Podcast Episode 331:** Snezana and Susanne – Happy Birthday, November 10, 2022
**Contact Information:** Instagram / Facebook: @Snezana Radojicic, Ciklonomad

# Laura Cozik

**Let's Travel Together and Have Fun!**

*"Don't follow the crowd, let the crowd follow you."*
- Margaret Baroness Thatcher, British Stateswoman

Laura and I were introduced by Elizabeth Lim, a fellow super marathon runner and triathlete. It's amazing how sports bring people together.

Laura - I'm the CEO of **LeveledUp Experiences** and **Mallorca by Design.** These companies empower women to step out of their comfort zones and equip them with tools for extraordinary breakthroughs in life. It might sound pretty badass, and it is. Seeing women's confidence grow is incredibly fulfilling for me. I split my time between Mallorca, Spain, and New York City. The pandemic made things challenging, but travel is slowly making a comeback. It's great to see people enjoying exploring and experiencing the world again. I love creating unique experiences for others.

Laura is also the Founder of Team Lipstick, New York City's all-female triathlon team. Her impressive background spans 30 years of dancing and fitness coaching, 10 years as a nationally ranked ballroom dance champion, and 3 years as CNN's Athletic Director. Since 2006, she has been actively participating in triathlons. Notably, she trained

Nicole Kidman in New York until her relocation to Spain. Interacting with Laura radiates great and positive energy!

**The local experience and preparation:** I never take a group to a place I haven't visited and tested myself. Organizing these trips is my favorite part. For example, I spent 15 days in Morocco, exploring the entire country to find the best experiences for my audience. Planning every detail, from the welcome cocktail to the final celebration, is a lot of work, but it's worth it. We seek out unique, non-touristy experiences that make the trips special and surprising. We ask you to trust us and join the adventure. So, when I say, "Put on this headlamp and follow me to the van at nine o'clock at night," you say, "OK." This thorough preparation takes a lot of time, but it's worth it. I always try to work with women-owned hotels or villas. We always have exclusive accommodations, ensuring no one else is with us. That's one of our specialties. Additionally, we vet our participants. You must go through a process to join our events. Are you ready? Talk to her!

**What are the qualifications to join you?** In the past, we've turned away a few women because we seek those who say YES to adventures. We want women who are open to trying something new, willing to get a little uncomfortable, and who enjoy working out and training their bodies. It's about stepping up to the plate, pushing yourself in a new environment, and having fun.

**Come and join others if you:**
-   Want to achieve something in your career
-   Want to get on stage or speak to a room full of a thousand people
-   Want to do something epic but feel nervous
-   Aren't sure if you can do it
-   Want to meet like-minded women.

You need a circle of friends cheering you on, saying, **"You've got this, you can do this**." You need that push, that community, and the chance to build confidence in yourself. That's what we provide, and we do it well.

Everyone's been to **Tuscany,** but we find the little, special, magical spots just for you. In one of the villages we're visiting, there are only seventeen residents—it's tiny, but it's special. We love to surprise our guests. Some of the women already know that when they come with me, something extraordinary is in store. I love creating unforgettable surprises and delights that blow my guests away. A vacation should be your time to relax, escape, and disconnect. But it can also be your time to LevelUp and experience something new.

Are you ready? Join us to enjoy each other's company, share stories, forge new friendships, and have an insane amount of fun!

---

**Podcast Episode 141:** Laura Cozik – How to Dare – Founder of Team Lipstick, January 13, 2021
**Contact Information:** Instagram: @Teamlipsticknyc / https://www.mallorcabydesign.com/

## Marathon Swimming – a State of Mind

*"When someone tells me I cannot do something,
it's when I do it."*
- Gertrude Ederle, the first woman to swim the
English Channel

Shannon is a marathon swimmer and also a podcaster, (**"Marathon Swim Stories"**) which is how I met her. As a runner, I know that a marathon race is 26.2 miles. But swimming a marathon? That sounds crazy (at least for me)!

**What is marathon swimming?** Shannon - my favorite definition of a marathon swim is that it's a state of mind. Technically, it's considered a 10KM or longer swim, which amounts to roughly three hours. I started open water swimming in 2009. At the time, I was working in business intelligence for Microsoft. I grew up as a competitive pool swimmer in Colorado and didn't think much about open water. But by then, I was living in Vermont, where there was a lake in every town. We had just moved there recently, and I was trying to get back into shape and meet new people. I signed up for a one-mile open water swim at an event called Kingdom Swim. As I walked down to the beach for my event, I saw people coming out of the water who had been swimming all morning while I was eating breakfast and worrying about my event. They did a 10-mile open water swim. It took my breath away. I finished my one mile and immediately threw myself into learning what it takes to be a marathon swimmer. Next, I did three miles, then a 10KM in Bermuda in the saltwater, which was something new to me.

**It's a mindset:** One of the vivid memories I keep forever is day 3 of a 4-day, 40-mile lake swim in Arizona, at the start of the roughly 18-mile swim. I was terrified. The water was freezing. I had never swum this far before, and I thought maybe I had made a mistake. Then somebody said, "Have a great swim!" My heart leapt with joy. YES, let's enjoy a day out on the water doing what we love!

**What do you eat?** I'm a real food person; when I started open water swimming, I didn't want to rely on just powder mixed with water. I like real food! As a general rule, you need carbohydrates to keep your energy up, replenish electrolytes lost from sweating in the water, and on longer swims, you want to add some proteins to sustain you. The challenge started when I signed up for swims further afield. You can't always find what you have at home, or a blender to make your own smoothies. Eventually, I succumbed to just adding water powders for fuel, but there is always a point in the swim when I need solid, real food. Fortunately, grapes are pretty ubiquitous, and treats like cookies are always welcome. I have a standard feed plan and let my support person, the kayaker or crew on the boat, know if I want something different on my next feed. The boat slows down a little, giving me the opportunity to take a quick drink of fuel or have a snack.

**What do you think about on your long swims?** I think a lot about my technique. I let my mind wander and sometimes ponder on solving the world's problems. Marathon swimming connects me deeply with nature and the rhythms of the earth. Swimming into the night, I witness sunsets, moonsets, and the rise of stars. I observe constellations moving across the sky, feeling like I'm part of the earth's rotation. All my everyday worries wash away—it's truly awe-inspiring.

**Swimming at night:** It took me a while to get comfortable swimming at night—I was afraid! I recommend practicing with others before going solo. Typically, there's a kayak or boat with lights for safety. When we swim Lake Tahoe, we do it overnight to avoid traffic and wind. There are many benefits to night swimming, despite it being disorienting. During my 21-mile swim across Lake Tahoe, starting at 9 pm, I grew weary of the darkness after sunset. The boat lights blurred, making it hard to judge distance. Sometimes I'd drift off course, prompting the pilot to wave lights to regain my attention. I might have been sleep swimming! Finally, the first light of dawn brought immense relief. The sunrise gave me a renewed energy boost, like a second wind.

---

**Podcast Episode 227:** Shannon Keegan – The Marathon Swimmer, September 20, 2021
**Contact Information:** https://www.intrepidwater.com

# Ellen Waterston

## Nurturing Literary Creativity

*"A word after a word after a word is power."*
– Margaret Atwood, Canadian poet, novelist, literary critic,
essayist, teacher, environmental activist, and inventor

Ellen - I am a resident of Bend, Oregon, in the high desert area. I'm a poet, educator, speaker, and award-winning writer.

Ellen - offers amazing writers' retreats. I spent a week with her and a few other inspiring writers, just writing and exploring. Ellen always encourages everyone to try something new for themselves. She has led workshops in the United States and abroad.

I love teaching creative writing (and she makes it seem so easy!). It's just about turning on the light switch because people have so much inside that needs to be expressed. I created **"The Writing Ranch"** to offer retreats and workshops for emerging and established writers. The "established writer" part is misleading because we're all emerging and beginning all the time. Whatever we do creatively, there's always the equivalent of the blank page each day.
I'd say we're all beginning and emerging every day. We all start at the same point. We might not finish at the same point or at the same time, but we all start with the same blank page.

**Have you always been a writer?**
I believe our childhood experiences greatly shape our creative paths. Being the youngest in my family, I often felt more isolated than my siblings. They formed their own unit. I remember writing in small, pink, plastic-covered diaries. It wasn't until ninth or tenth grade that I realized my words could vividly convey scenes, movements, and emotions.

From then on, I became deeply immersed in writing. I pursued it in various forms, including writing for my college paper. Journalism became my initial career path, allowing me to travel extensively while working for Skiing magazine in Europe.

After moving West, getting married, and ranching, I started writing for local newspapers. Eventually, I focused on expanding my own creative endeavors, particularly poetry, which I've been writing for many years. Alongside my poetry, I've founded two nonprofit organizations dedicated to literary arts, in addition to establishing The Writing Ranch as its educational branch.

Excerpt from her book "*Walking the High Desert: Encounters with Rural America along the Oregon Desert Trail*" (June 2020):

*"Former high desert rancher Ellen Waterston writes about a rugged, largely untouched, and strikingly beautiful region of the American West. She takes on a creative and*

*curious journey along the newly established 750-mile Oregon Desert Trail, introducing readers to a desert characterized as 'trusting, naïve, earnest, stubbly, grumpy old man' grappling with pressing national and global issues. These include public land use, livestock grazing rights, safeguarding sacred Indigenous sites, water rights, and protecting habitats for endangered species."*

Loving writing can seem odd, especially for someone active like an athlete, because it involves long periods of sitting. In her spare time, she values staying active, with cross-country skiing being particularly important to her.

---

**Podcast Episode 87:** Ellen Waterston - Writing Ranch, Walking the High Desert - Bend, Oregon
**Contact Information:** https://www.writingranch.com/

# Janet Wise

## Dress for Success, always!

*"When you don't dress like everybody else, you don't have
to think like everybody else."*
- Iris Apfel, American businesswoman,
interior & fashion designer

Janet - I love her fitting name because she always has wise advice for ambitious women who are thriving and managing their careers.

Janet brings a wealth of experience from her 20+ years in corporate career and talent management, leadership, and learning and development at Fortune 50 companies, as well as from launching her own company. She firmly believes that you are the most important product you will ever market. I met her through Gloria Stevens (we'll get to know her later) when she offered sophisticated learning and networking lunches for women in New York City.

Her husband commented on her elegant work attire: "I was working from home even before the pandemic and realized early on that for my productivity, mindset, engagement, and enjoyment, I needed to dress for success. Sure, I could be in my PJs or sweats for a while, but that wasn't what energized me. What energizes me is positivity and self-confidence. A positive self-image inspires optimism and productivity. When you take the time to present yourself in the best way, you're essentially working from the outside in. There is an inner boost when I am well-presented. Dress for yourself first! It signals to your heart and energy that you will be effective and successful. Today and every day, I'm going to work with this mantra."

**Be Branded. Be Brilliant. Be You.**

How you present yourself at work, along with the work you produce, shapes your career brand. I'm going to be brilliant on brand, and I'll show the world how to do it too.

**Wise Career Advice:**
1. **Dress for the Role You Aspire To:** Elevate your professional appearance by dressing for the position you aim to achieve. Adding a touch of lipstick can enhance your confidence and presence in any outfit!
2. **Maintain a Professional Virtual Presence:** Ensure your video call backdrop is tidy and professional. Avoid including personal spaces like unmade beds to keep the focus on you!
3. **Show Up for Yourself and Your Team:** Actively engage with your work and colleagues. This commitment will boost your impact, empowerment, and credibility.
4. **Recognize Ongoing Challenges and Resilience:** Acknowledge that balancing multiple roles and increased workloads, especially for women, remains challenging in the post pandemic world. Continue to navigate these demands with resilience, empathy, and adaptability.

5. **Always Use Video in Virtual Meetings:** Being on camera increases your visibility and presence in virtual settings, making you more memorable and engaged. As they say – out of sight, out of mind.
6. **Practice Active Listening:** Enhance your communication by listening actively, even when it's more challenging in a virtual environment.
7. **Craft a Compelling Personal Message:** Develop a strong personal brand statement for times when hiring decisions, succession planning, or promotions occur without your presence, or for use at networking events.
8. **Communicate Clearly and Concisely:** Be able to articulate your strengths and accomplishments in brief, impactful sound bites that can represent you when you're not there.
9. **Understand Your Unique Attributes:** Identify and leverage your personal strengths and how they align with your career goals or the values of a new organization.

**What is your superpower and way of working?**
"I will not create your brand, but I will help you reveal it. I will do it in a New York minute—not because it's easy, but because it's easy for me to see that in you."

---

**Podcast Episode April 183:** Janet Wise – What is YOUR Superpower - Chief Career Strategist, April 26, 2021
**Contact Information:** Instagram: @Janet Wise – Wise Advantages

# Nighat Shah

## A Passionate Champion for Mental Health

*"I am a woman. I am successful.*
*And I am not afraid to speak my mind.*
*And that doesn't sit well with a lot of men – and women."*
– Sharmeen Obaid Chinoy, Oscar winning filmmaker


Nighat - originally from Pakistan, but now she and her family live in Memphis, TN. When do you ever meet a TEDx Speaker and a successful film producer via your friends Gloria and Caroline? It's about networking and bringing the right, amazing women together. This is how it should be in life: we support each other and lift each other up.

Nighat has an impressive background as a film producer, impact investor, and humanitarian. I started my film production company a few years ago. I try to help wherever help is needed; wherever I can be of help, I am there.

I care deeply about advocating for better mental health care in Pakistan and globally. This passion drove me to create my first short film, **"This Bank of the River."** In the years leading up to its production, I became increasingly concerned about the rising suicide rates in my hometown of Chitral. As a tight-knit community where families have lived for generations, each loss of life deeply affected our social fabric. Sadly, these incidents were becoming more frequent, affecting vulnerable youth and elders alike.

**What can we do?**
To address the challenge, I started providing seminars, but soon realized they were ineffective because they primarily reached individuals who were already aware and concerned about mental health issues. Recognizing the need for broader awareness, I aimed to elevate the discussion in Pakistan's mainstream media. My goal was to encourage open dialogue about mental health and urge policymakers to invest in better mental health facilities.

Given the remote and inaccessible mountainous regions of Pakistan where mental health support is scarce, I created the film "This Bank of the River" ("Darya Kay Iss Paar"). The film's narrative revolves around a river where many suicides occur, symbolizing the profound impact of these tragic events on our community.

**How do you envision reaching the mountainous region?**
My vision for reaching the mountainous region involves using "This Bank of the River" as a provocative tool to raise awareness about the prevalent issue of suicide in these areas. The film aims to shed light on why women, young children, and youth are taking their lives, seeking to uncover the root causes and identify preventive measures. By bringing this issue to the forefront, my goal is to prompt Pakistan's national media to engage in discussions about mental health openly and supportively, breaking the taboo surrounding it. It's about fostering a culture of mutual support and understanding, where mental health is addressed openly rather than kept in secrecy.

**What have you learned from your parents?**
Adur is my mother's name. It comes from Persian, referring to qualities of strength, character and kindness - traits that defined my mother and still inspire the compassionate storytelling I pursue through my production company Adur.

- I named my company after my mother: **ADUR.** She's incredibly kind yet assertive, and she knows how to get things done.
- My childhood was different. My parents raised me to be a **problem solver.** Especially my father always involved me and my siblings in discussions about challenges so we could work together to find solutions.
- In Pakistan, where I'm from, women and girls are often expected to do kitchen work. But my parents ensured we had a well-rounded upbringing.

I owe everything to my parents.

**Fast forward** to 2024, Nighat's feature narrative **"Gunjal"** (Entangled) brings to life the inspiring story of Iqbal Masih, a child labor activist who passionately fought for the freedom of bonded child laborers. The film has been screened at numerous prestigious festivals, amplifying Iqbal's voice and sparking inspiration for change.

---

**Podcast Episode 230:** Nighat Shah – Mental Health in Pakistan, September 27, 2021
**Contact Information:** www.adurproduction.com

# Agnes Hirschi

## Kindness amidst Bombardment

*"Think of all the beauty still left around you and be happy."*
– Anne Frank, German Jewish Girl

Agnes - a dear family friend, shares her story of survival during World War II in Budapest, Hungary. As a young girl, along with her mother and Swiss diplomat Carl Lutz, she endured two months in a bomb shelter.

My parents were Hungarian Jews living in Budapest, Hungary. We enjoyed a comfortable life; my father was a prosperous businessman. We resided in a beautiful apartment near the parliament, had a housekeeper, and had the means to travel. Concerned by the political developments in Europe, my father decided to emigrate to Great Britain. He sent my eight-month pregnant mother to London, where I was born. His foresight led me to become a British citizen, a strategic move for our safety. Shortly after my birth, however, we returned to Budapest.

**Carl Lutz,** born in 1895 in Walzenhausen, Switzerland, was the second youngest of ten children. At a young age, he ventured to the United States with no money, no knowledge of English, and no connections. He studied at George Washington University in Washington, DC, and after graduating, he worked for the Swiss Legation. After twenty years in the US, Lutz returned to Switzerland in 1935, married, and was assigned to Palestine. His time in Palestine held deep religious significance for him as it was the biblical land. When World War II began, he represented German interests, a role that later proved pivotal in Budapest, Hungary. In January 1942, he and his wife relocated to Budapest, where life initially remained relatively normal; people could still attend theaters, enjoy coffee along the Danube River, and visit the famous thermal baths. Lutz, a skilled photographer, captured these moments. Everything changed dramatically after the German invasion on March 19, 1944, particularly for Jews. Overnight, they lost their rights, were forced to wear yellow stars, and could no longer freely walk the streets. Within hours, severe restrictions were imposed, and their personal belongings were confiscated.

Carl Lutz, then head of the department of foreign interest of the Swiss Legation in Budapest, represented the interests of fourteen countries during the war, including Great Britain and the United States. Following the German invasion of Budapest, he retained authority to legally send 7,800 Jews to Palestine. Lutz, deeply religious, felt a moral obligation to help these people and found a way: he offered Swiss protection to Jews awaiting emigration to Palestine. To maximize the number of people he could protect, Lutz cleverly interpreted Adolf Eichmann's directives, defining a "unit" as a family rather than individuals. This tactic allowed him to significantly increase the number of people under Swiss protection; a family of six, for example, counted as just one "unit." It's estimated that Lutz saved around 50,000 lives through these efforts, risking both his life and career in the process.

**How did you endure those difficult times?** During those challenging days, my beautiful mother and I lived near the former American Legation, where Carl Lutz's office was based. Through a series of events, my mother was hired as a housekeeper in Lutz's residence in Buda. After Christmas in 1944, the bombings became so intense that we sought refuge in bomb shelters. My makeshift bed was two large chairs pushed together; We were among about thirty people, anxiously waiting for the war to end.

One poignant memory stands out: my seventh birthday on January 3rd, 1945, celebrated in the bomb shelter with a precious treat of white chocolate and watery cocoa that Lutz had saved for the occasion. His efforts to bring some joy to that day are something I will never forget.

Agnes speaks passionately about this topic and has shared her experiences in numerous talks around the world.

---

**Podcast Episode 28:** Agnes Hirschi - Surviving in Budapest in the Bomb Shelter, March 17, 2020
**Contact Information:** www.carl-lutz.com
**Book Information:** "Under Swiss Protection - Jewish Eyewitness accounts from Wartime Budapest" by Agnes Hirschi and Charlotte Schallié (2017)
**Film:** "Carl Lutz – the Forgotten Hero" by Daniel von Aarburg.

# LISTENING

*"We don't need to share the same opinions as others,*
*but we need to be respectful."*
- Taylor Swift, American Singer

Listening carefully is a crucial characteristic in your leadership journey. Being present and aware are often overlooked but essential elements.

In today's world, with smartphones, TVs, computers, and social media constantly vying for our attention, true listening can be overshadowed by a constant stream of information. Truly hearing the real story requires us to pause, focus, and engage deeply with others.

**When have you listened carefully? Where do you listen carefully?**
In nature, practicing forest bathing, as the Japanese call this well-being technique, allows us to harmonize with our natural surroundings and disconnect from the outside world.

Even in bustling places like airports or city centers, amid the cacophony of noise that bombards our senses, there's an opportunity to listen deeply. These environments offer a contrast that can sharpen our ability to focus on the essential, filtering out distractions to hear life's meaningful lessons and stories that demand our undivided attention.

# Destiny Jae Cool

## Discovering connections through curiosity

*"It is not how much we do,*
*but how much love we put in the doing."*
- Mother Teresa

Destiny - I'm currently studying Creative Technology and Design Engineering at the University of Colorado Boulder. After I graduate, I want to work in the adaptive technology industry to assist people with disabilities.

**What do we have in common?**
We both serve on the board of Advisors for EDsnaps. For several years, I've been an e-counselor with EDsnaps, focusing on supporting underrepresented young women aged 12-18. During the pandemic, I had the chance to connect with these students online, which was a valuable experience facilitated by technology. Some of them were from the Bronx, New York, and Chicago, while I also engaged in projects with girls in Ghana, Africa. Coming from a small town near Denver, I didn't have such global exposure growing up. EDsnaps has taught me how to empower female students, helping them discover confidence in themselves and their STEM abilities.

**How did you get interested in STEM?**
I originally wanted to pursue a career in politics, aiming to work for the Pentagon and studying law to become a lawyer. However, my path took a different turn one summer when I worked as a lifeguard at a local pool. I witnessed a little boy, just five years old, who had two prosthetic legs. Despite his challenges, he interacted with other kids joyfully and was the happiest among them. His resilience deeply impressed and moved me. This experience motivated me to delve into the world of prosthetics. To work in that field, I realized I needed to study engineering to understand the materials involved in creating prosthetics.

**What were your learning moments?**
Before my involvement with EDsnaps, I used to be reluctant to ask questions, seeing it as something discouraged or a sign of not paying attention or understanding. However, participating in EDsnaps programs has transformed me, making me more curious and confident. I learned from Susanne Mueller, particularly from her podcast episodes where she asks insightful questions to amazing people, recording their stories and fostering lasting relationships. Through this, I realized that asking questions isn't just about seeking information but also about listening closely and building connections.

**Networking:**
I attended the Society of Women Engineers Conference in fall 2021 and felt terrified because I didn't know how to ask questions or connect with people.

Now, I rely on these questions when meeting new people:

- Where are you from?
- What are you studying?
- What do you do for work?
- What do you enjoy most about your job?
- How did you become interested in your field?
- Where do you see yourself after graduation?
- What more can I learn from you?
- Is there anything else you'd like to share?

I've learned that it's important to dig deeper into people's stories. It's crucial to approach conversations with positivity, gratitude, and appreciation for the time experts spend with me. My big "AHA" moment came when I realized that active listening is the key.

**What do you do when you don't work? (or study)**
When I'm not working or studying, I make a conscious effort to unwind. I've learned not to stress over everything. One of my favorite ways to relax is hiking or simply being in nature. I also enjoy crocheting, whether it's creating my own projects or making gifts for others.

---

**Podcast Episode 259:** Destiny Cool – What is your Question? December 27, 2021
**Contact Information**: www.edsnaps.org

# Gloria M. Stevens

## Bold Hats for a Bold Lifestyle

*"Find out who you are and do it on purpose."*
- Dolly Parton, singer, songwriter, and philanthropist


Gloria and I have known each other since our days studying Psychology at Marymount Manhattan College in New York. We used to take the bus home together in the evenings and later pursued our Master's Degrees in Organizational Development and Leadership at Columbia University. After graduating, Gloria became the President of the Psychology Society Association (PSYA), a group of female psychology alumni dedicated to providing leadership and mentorship to Psychology college students. Studying later in life created a strong, lifelong bond between us.

Gloria - now is the perfect moment to reinvent ourselves and prepare for new adventures. Over the years, both Gloria and I have undergone numerous experiences that have led us to reinvent ourselves.

Gloria has always had a passion for hats, which inspired her to create the program **"Hats in Time."** This program revolves around the 3C concept: Caps, Coffee, and Conversation. We all wear many hats in life, and this metaphor forms the core of her life coaching program. Each month, Gloria features a different hat in a blog post along with a book she's currently reading. These selections serve as inspiration for others to start meaningful conversations.

**Have you always been wearing hats?**
Since I have met Gloria, she has always worn a hat that suits every situation and occasion with elegance. Hats have become my way of connecting with people. While researching for my blog, I found a photo of myself with my sister wearing a cowboy hat when I was about two years old. Since then, hats have been my trademark in every business I've led. They give me confidence and make me feel ready to face the world. Choosing the right hat for each occasion completes my outfit perfectly. Hats are my joy and they embody my identity, no matter what life brings.

**How many hats do you have?**
I have an impressive collection of about 260 hats right now, even though I live in a one-room apartment in New York City. My place is filled with shelves stacked with hat boxes, and I even have a rotating hat tree for different seasons like spring and winter styles. I've curated hats for every day of the year, ranging from various caps, fedoras, and berets to elegant wide-rimmed hats for weddings and practical straw hats with nets from the early automobile era.

Each hat holds a special story from where and how I acquired it. One of my recent favorites is an Opera hat—a collapsible top hat that came in its original box. Because my friends know my passion for hats, they often gift me hats for my birthday or Christmas.

Recently, a friend inherited a collection of hats from an estate and passed them on to me, adding to my collection. For me, hats are not just accessories; they're a part of celebrating life's occasions in style and with history.

**What is the program all about?**
The **"Hats in Time"** program, centered around the **3Cs— Caps, Coffee, and Conversation**—is designed to empower individuals through personalized coaching and meaningful dialogue:

1. **Caps:** Let's put a cap on that works for you: This involves finding the right metaphorical "cap" or approach that suits your goals and aspirations.
2. **Coffee:** Let's have a conversation first to get to know each other: This phase focuses on building a connection and understanding your thoughts, goals, and concerns:
3. **Conversation:**
   - What are your thoughts?
   - Where are you headed?
   - What keeps you up at night?

**A real Success story:**
I've had the privilege of supporting an individual through our conversations as she pursued her goals, becoming more adventurous and fulfilling her dream of starting a business in a new country.

Her testimonial captures the impact of our work together:

*"I wouldn't have had the confidence to make such a bold lifestyle change without Gloria's advice and support."*

"Life's Journey – Wearing many Hats"

---

**Podcast Episode 319:** Gloria Stevens – Life Coaching – Hats in Time – A Hat for each Occasion, November 13, 2023
**Contact Information:** https://www.hatsintime.com/

# Caroline Sposto

## Unlocking Human Connection

*"I was raised to be an independent woman,
not the victim of anything."*
- Kamala Harris, first female Vice President,
United States of America


Caroline - I've always been fascinated by human communication. I've worked as a writer, editor, and adjunct professor. Now, I run a business called **Savvy Civility**, which I started in 2018. We met over a glass of wine at a local diner in New York City with Gloria. Sharing stories and uplifting each other connected us.

**What is your business?**
We send actors across the United States for education and research purposes. Think of it like learning to fly a plane. First, you study everything on paper. They wouldn't put you in the cockpit right away because mistakes could be disastrous. Instead, they use a flight simulator where you can practice flying in different conditions and stressful situations safely. You learn from your mistakes in a controlled environment before eventually flying a real plane.

**How does it work?**
I have a pool of trained actors that I send to medical schools. The students know they're dealing with actors but don't know what the medical case will be. Professors rate the

students on their ability to gather the patient's medical history. The actors play difficult or unusual personalities, then break character to give the students interpersonal feedback. Good bedside manners are crucial!

Students learn in a safe but stressful environment. They might make mistakes with the actors, such as misdiagnosing or mishandling a situation, but they learn what not to do in real clinical settings. I write the scenarios, and the actors study their roles, with some improvisation since the medical students aren't following a script.

There is always an element of surprise in our simulations. Once, we did a training in Arizona where the actors wore prison uniforms instead of regular clothes. The students knew they were actors, but we had the actors act a bit more aggressively. In real life, students never know what kind of patients they will encounter and treat.

In another simulation, the actors dressed as homeless people with dirty clothes and hair. We even added special effects makeup to make them look like they had sores. It was a fun challenge. Nowadays, as a medical student, you have to be prepared to treat people from all walks of life and be ready for any situation. They must be comfortable helping anyone.

**What was the moment when you knew to start your business?**
In 2008, my sister was terminally ill, and she had many friends who wanted to spend time with her during her final days. The room was always filled with positive energy,

laughter, and love. One day, a doctor came in and, for some reason, felt that the uplifting atmosphere was wrong. He made a negative comment, and after he left, the mood in the room dropped. My sister stopped talking, and shortly after, she fell into a coma and passed away.

That moment made me realize the power of positive environments and inspired me to start my business. That moment gave me the motivation to start my own company. Why not? My focus is on providing medical actors to smaller programs or colleges that lack big resources. The schools I serve are typically for physician assistant, nurse practitioner, and physical therapist programs, but not full MD schools since they usually have in-house setups.

Bedside manners matter! They can be trained with actors.

---

**Podcast Episode 311:** Caroline Sposto – Interpersonal Communication Training, July 4, 2023
**Contact Information:** https://www.savvycivility.com/

# Nanci France-Vaz

## Balancing Success as an Artist and Businesswoman

*"I didn't know what I wanted to do,
but I always knew the woman I wanted to be."*
- Diane von Furstenberg, fashion designer


### Figurative Storyteller

"As a painter, my primary goal is to capture the essence of the human experience, drawing inspiration from film, poetry, and classic literature while infusing contemporary themes. In a world that often feels emotionally distant, my aim is to evoke a deep response from viewers by depicting the psychological nuances and moods of my subjects within their environments. Human beings are complex, with layers shaped by both past experiences and current realities, constantly evolving from one form or idea to another." - Nanci France-Vaz

Nanci - when I was about five years old, I remember watching an Elvis Presley movie. At that moment, I knew I wanted to be an actress and dancer, to become famous. I loved writing and reading stories—I'd go to the library and devour plays, memorizing every line with my photographic memory. I'd make costumes and perform in our living room. Teachers encouraged me in acting, and later, I competed in gymnastics. Theatre, dance, and painting were my passions! Despite trying different jobs, even Wall Street, to please my parents, I was unhappy, even depressed, turning to drugs. All I really wanted was to be an artist!

At thirty-six, a friend suggested, "Why don't you go to art school? You're always doodling and sketching." I wondered if it was too late at my age. Without any prior drawing classes, I had to assemble fifteen pieces for a portfolio review. Balancing a full-time job, I took two night classes. Determined to become an artist and get into SVA in New York, I worked tirelessly on weekends and evenings. Within three months, I had my portfolio ready and was accepted. They transferred 36 credits from Brooklyn College, and the rest is history.

My teacher and mentor once told me, "You're tenacious, you don't give up, you have talent, and you're my best student!" I learned computer animation for film and special effects, skills that now benefit my Instagram reels and marketing materials. My confidence in front of the camera, fueled by my passion for acting, has also been a tremendous asset.

Managing student loans had its challenges, but I refused to give up. Despite ups and downs, my dedication eventually paid off. A few years ago, one of my portraits was selected for one of the world's most prestigious shows.

As self-made millionaire Ed McNamee, who owned his own finance company, once said, "There are six key elements to being successful:

- **Desire**
- **Determination**
- **Drive**
- **Focus**
- **Persistence**
- **Passion.**

When you possess all these qualities, it no longer feels like work."

**Fast forward to 2024:** From July to September 2024, Nanci will be at a summer residence at the Nerdrum School in Norway.

---

**Podcast Episode 297:** Nanci France – Think like a Business Person, April 6, 2022
**Contact Information:** https://www.nancifrancevaz.com

# Yvonne Lucrezia Condrau

## Dreams Unfolded: A Storyteller's Journey

*"Perseverance is failing 19 times
and succeeding on the 20th."*
- Julie Andrews, actress

Yvonne Condrau and I are both originally from Switzerland. We met while working at the Swiss Mission to the United Nations, grateful for our jobs at such a prestigious office in New York. Despite this, these roles weren't our dream careers. Sometimes, we must patiently wait for our dream jobs to materialize. It's essential to never give up, dream big, and strive to make it happen.

Yvonne - had always dreamed of coming to the United States. In 1993, she finally moved to New York City with plans to stay for a year or two. However, fate intervened when she met her husband, who is from New York City, and she never left.

**What were your dreams?**
Well, I had many dreams, but one of my biggest was to become a storyteller and writer someday. Even as a young girl, I could create captivating stories out of thin air and had a knack for writing and languages. I've always been passionate about reading books and writing. When I was younger, I exchanged numerous letters with an uncle in

Canada—he wanted to practice his German, and I wanted to improve my English.

In my teenage years, I began writing a novel, but unfortunately, I discarded whatever pages I wrote. It was during a lunch with Yvonne that I suggested she take advanced screenplay writing classes at New York University. This suggestion sparked a new beginning! Sometimes, all it takes is one person to nudge you forward. I'm glad to have been that person and to be on this journey with you!

**Learning:**
Writing screenplays turned out to be much tougher than I anticipated. I'm grateful I invested in specialized software like Final Draft because the Hollywood industry is incredibly strict and demanding. There are countless rules to follow, and the software truly helps in adhering to them. In film, actions and dialogues won't translate if scenes aren't meticulously described, portrayed, explained, or illustrated in detail—the key principle being "show, don't tell."

I paused work on my first script, "Domino Effect" (Drama/Mystery), to assist a friend in writing my debut feature screenplay, **"A Scottish Gem"** (Drama/Romance). This script is based on the book and true story "Carole's Story… A Scottish Gem," written by Michele M. Rodger in December 2010. Little did I realize, choosing to adapt a true story made my path even more challenging, as it required me to stay faithful to the original narrative while also nurturing my creativity.

Adapting Michele's first book, which tells a compelling story about her unique sister-in-law in Scotland—a true gem—was quite a challenge. The book spans 328 pages, but my task was to condense the essence into approximately one hundred pages for a drama screenplay. This process highlighted why movies often can't capture all the nuances of a book. I've spent nearly two years editing, often waking up with new ideas to tweak scenes repeatedly.

For both first-time and seasoned writers, there are numerous competitions, contests, and film festivals available. I've submitted my script to many of these, and through persistent hard work, I've been fortunate to receive several awards and honorable mentions. These include recognition from Swiss Screenwriting and Cinematic Summit, Humro Cinema FF in Nepal, Edinburgh Film Awards, New Wave-International Script & Film Festival in Berlin, London Movie Awards, New York Movie Awards, City of Angels Women's FF in California, and more.

**Wisdom - Biggest Learning**

Just never give up! Despite facing numerous setbacks, I believe every failure is an opportunity to grow and learn. It's like in sports: "You win today, lose tomorrow, but always get back on your feet and never give up." There were days, even weeks, when I stared at a blank page unable to write anything.

As my Instagram bio states: "15-time Award-winning Screenwriter of Best Unproduced Feature Screenplay."

Now, all I need is a producer who believes in the success of "A Scottish Gem!"

Good luck to all of us—see you in Hollywood at the Oscars!

Remember to "Be Bold, Brave & Brilliant!"

---

**Podcast Episode 178:** Yvonne Condrau – See you in Hollywood, a Screenplay Writer's Journey, April 10, 2021
**Contact Information:** Instagram:
@yvonnecondrau_screenwriter_usa

# Cristina Bertarelli

## Crafting a Creative Career

*"We need to reshape our own perception of how we view ourselves. We have to step up as women and take the lead."*
- Beyoncé, singer


Cristina and I met through the New York University Coaching program with many things in common like coaching, traveling, and curiosity with living away from our home countries in Europe.

Cristina – is a coach, a creative, and a fun-loving Italian woman who's been a globetrotter for over 20 years, living in various places worldwide. My creative spirit was quiet for a long time, but there's beauty in waiting. Now, I feel like a late bloomer with a lively soul.

Last summer, Cristina, instead of flying back home to New York after my daughter's graduation in the UK, we decided to take the Queen Mary 2 transatlantic ocean liner. The accommodations were top-notch, and the service was impeccable. The ship offered elegant tea ceremonies, making our journey feel luxurious and stylish despite the rainy, foggy weather throughout. To pass the time, I attended fascinating art lectures and read extensively. Then, I decided to try something completely new: a watercolor class. I had never painted before in my life and found myself just mixing colors without a clue where to begin. Surprisingly, I enjoyed it. The teacher even encouraged me to continue painting after the trip. I wondered, what did he see in me?

Back in New York, as I unpacked, I stumbled upon my notebook. Remembering the encouragement from the watercolor class teacher, I promptly enrolled in a class at the Art Students League. During introductions, I openly admitted my lack of painting experience and expressed my eagerness to learn. Starting with simple stripes and experimenting with color mixing, I began to see surprising results. It was immensely enjoyable—a time of exploration without pressure, simply absorbing the experience. Once again, the teacher praised my efforts, saying, "You have an eye for it!" This affirmation spurred me on, and I committed to attending weekly classes, starting with once a week.

**Your art sold at your first exhibition:** It was a lottery for students in the fall program. Out of five hundred pieces, mine was chosen to be shown at the year-end exhibition. I felt incredibly fortunate, especially since I had only completed four small pieces at that point. Choosing which one to exhibit was tough because I was quite attached to all of them. I attended the exhibition with my friends, and it turned out to be a delightful evening. While there, I received a call from the school informing me that my piece had been sold. Overwhelmed with emotion, I burst into tears. The experience still moves me deeply.

Then the school asked me to bring another piece to fill the space on the wall. It was a significant moment for me, filled with a mix of emotions—happiness and overwhelming feelings. When I replaced the sold piece, I brought my family along, as my kids were eager to see the exhibition. We made it a special trip to explore the other artworks on display. Seeing my family with me made me realize how much joy I found in sharing my art, despite my naturally shy nature. You once gave me a book by Herminia Ibarra, which taught me the importance of embracing imperfection rather than striving for perfection. That lesson resonates deeply with where I am now.

**What's next?** I'm transitioning from drawing on paper to painting on canvas, which feels like a significant step. Recently, I finished a painting that surprised me—it turned out completely different from my original plan. The main theme was "Hope," inspired by current global events. I started with a background of a large white cloud. In the foreground, I envisioned a mix of nature against a cityscape with skyscrapers. As I worked, I added dots of color and included a pink reflection in the water, along with some blue. I titled this piece "Distractions Punto e Basta, number one."

An artist in the making – Looking forward to more! Congratulations!

---

**Podcast Episode 408**: Cristina Bertarelli – Late Bloomer, Vibrant Soul, February 26, 2024
**Contact Information:** Instagram: @Cristina Bertarelli_Art

# Michelle Nodiff

## A Voice of Joy and Warmth

*"Don't you ever let a soul in the world tell you that you can't be exactly who you are."* – Lady Gaga, singer, songwriter

Michelle - has the most pleasant, lovely voice. She's enjoyable to be around, whether at work or outside of it. I had a great time working with her. During our conversation, Michelle was transitioning between roles. We talked about her passions, which include voiceover work, teaching meditation, and crocheting.

**How did you discover all those hidden hobbies you never had time for?**
I've been going through a major career change. In my previous job, I was always incredibly busy and never had time for much else. Slowing down and stepping back has been challenging. During this transition, I focused on giving my mind some breathing room. I started learning how to crochet using online tutorials and websites. I ended up making several gifts for friends and family during the holidays. Crocheting has become a passion of mine, although now I have more yarn than I can fit in my small New York City apartment. (Since then, I've moved to a larger space outside New York City — we might need to check in on whether my yarn collection has grown even more!)

To keep from getting too bored, I enrolled in an online meditation teacher program. I'm sure that with my soothing voice, my meditation sessions will be a wonderful way to relax, dream, and follow along with my guidance.

**Voiceover: How did you get into this?**
I've been told for a while that I have a great voice suited for voiceover work. But it's more than just having a good voice. You have to fully embody the character, be authentic, believable, and evoke emotions in your audience. After receiving this feedback multiple times, I decided to enroll in a bootcamp with a company where I worked closely with a coach in personal sessions. This experience eventually led me to create my demo.

Thanks to my wonderful spouse, who graciously designed a beautiful website for me, I'm officially in business now. I've also upgraded my microphone, a crucial tool for my work. Voiceover encompasses a variety of fascinating niches, such as:
- Corporate e-learning and videos / Promos and trailers
- Telephony (press 1, press 2 when you call a call center)
- TV and film narrations, gaming, and audiobooks
- Character voices for tours, trade shows, and more

**My dream:**
It would be a dream come true to land a national commercial where my voice becomes synonymous with the brand for

years to come. When that day arrives, your support means the world to me!

I'm not limiting myself to just one thing; there are so many incredible areas to explore. When I first started, I didn't realize the breadth of opportunities available. Over the past few months, I've immersed myself like a sponge, diving into every aspect of voiceover.

**Fast forward:** I've taken on a significant role in HR leadership and attended two major voiceover conferences. After receiving coaching and completing a new commercial demo, I'm confident that one day you'll hear my voice and recognize it as that of a friend.

**From my website**: "From corporate narration and e-learning to commercials and video games, my voice offers a warm, friendly, reassuring tone that is soothing and perfectly suited for any audience."

---

**Podcast Episode 273:** Michelle Nodiff - the Best Voice for Voiceover and Meditation, February 7, 2022
**Contact Information:** https://www.michellenodiff.com/

# Silvana Gonzalez

## Coffee and the Circular Economy - Café La Divisa

*"The difference between successful people and others is how long they spend time feeling sorry for themselves."*
– Barbara Corcoran, real estate mogul, Shark tank investor

Silvana and I met at the Vital Voices conference in Washington, DC, where she kindly offered me a little Cafecito one early afternoon.

Silvana - the founder of **Café La Divisa** in Bogota, Colombia. It's Colombia's first global luxury coffee brand, now available in over eight countries. Our coffee is celebrated for its magical flavors, crafted with a deep commitment to sustainability and a passion for supporting our planet, its people, and women everywhere.

**History:** In Colombia, coffee is everything, as you know. Originally, I trained as a horse veterinarian. It's quite a surprise when I introduce myself - from horses to coffee. This shift is significant because I've always pursued my dreams since I was a little girl. Working with horses was my lifelong passion. Little did I know, pursuing that career meant delayed payments or chasing after my money. I was driving 5,000 kilometers per month and working at least 12 hours each day. Working long hours never bothered me, but not getting paid did. Then, I was robbed - cheated out of about 5,000 USD. That's a lot of money, and it was a massive wake-up call.

I was disciplined, committed, and passionate about my job, but I should have listened to my inner voice telling me something wasn't right. Sometimes, we need interventions from the universe. I felt sad, frustrated, scared, but the people around me said, "You can try anything, anything you want, now is the time."

Coffee has always been our family business. My father spent 40 years as a farmer, but producing food in developing countries is costly and demanding. Around that time, my brother was studying in Costa Rica and noticed families roasting their own coffee. He suggested we do the same, but we had no idea about product development, roasting, selling, or branding. We started anyway, only to discover the challenges of working in a family business. My brother eventually stepped down, and it was my turn to take charge, supported by my husband.

Initially, asserting myself and speaking up was tough, especially within my own family, where I wanted to show respect. But the greatest challenges bring the greatest rewards. Today, the company is entirely mine, and I lead it my way.

**Recycling program:** We aim to make a significant impact through our commitment to exceptional quality and luxury, alongside a strong focus on sustainability for the future. Our mission aligns closely with the United Nations Sustainable

Development Goals.One of our key challenges was what to do with used coffee bags once our customers were done with them. Working with major clients like Grand Hyatt and BMW in Colombia, we implemented a solution: when delivering the next order, customers return their used coffee bags to us. These bags are then transformed responsibly through a partnership with a local community into beautiful handbags and purses. This initiative embodies the circular economy at its best - producing, using, and then upcycling or recycling materials for further use. Moreover, the profits from these products are reinvested back into supporting that community.

This approach not only enhances our sustainability efforts but also fosters community empowerment and environmental stewardship, reflecting our commitment to making a positive impact at every stage of our business.

**What services do you offer?**
We offer a range of services beyond coffee itself. Alongside our premium coffee offerings, we provide corporate and social event services. As CEO, I enjoy personally overseeing our brewing stations at these events, which is how we initially connected at the Washington, DC conference. In our service line, we collaborate with various groups of women who bring their expertise in coffee or who we train from scratch. We believe in fair compensation and pay well, seeing it as essential in our leadership philosophy. "Income is freedom," as I firmly believe, underscores our commitment to valuing and empowering those who work with us.

These efforts not only ensure top-quality experiences for our clients but also contribute to our broader mission of promoting sustainability and supporting women in the coffee industry.

**Some of her wisdom:**
- Life will always be in flow
- Smiling is crucial for overall wellbeing
- Work-life balance is essential for work-life success.

---

**Podcast Episode 378**: Silvana Gonzalez – CEO and Co-Founder, Café La Divisa, August 21, 2023
**Contact Information:** https://cafeladivisa.com/

**Rediscovering Joy - Bringing PLAY back in your Life**

*"Champions keep playing until they get it right."*
- Billie Jean King, tennis player, activist

Brandi and I first crossed paths in 2019 when we both embarked on our podcasting journeys. It feels like just yesterday since we started. We were full of inspiration, eager to make our voices heard.

Since then, I've continued to share that same voice, unchanged. My professional journey has undergone significant shifts—from college professor to entrepreneur and now as a solo entrepreneur. Despite these changes, my core mission remains steadfast. Over the past six years, I've transitioned from teaching disability inclusion in sports, recreation, and play to becoming a professional speaker and entrepreneur. Throughout this evolution, one belief has remained constant: I firmly believe that play is crucial for our personal and professional health, growth, and connections.

At its core, **return to play** allows us to embrace our courage, creativity, and capabilities. Research underscores that during play, we are more inclusive, open to diverse ideas, adept at finding solutions, and authentically ourselves. However, understanding how people engage in play is essential.

**Your glamorous website:**
Your glamorous website may receive compliments like, "Your website is beautiful!" However, websites and social media represent our show home life—appearing flawless on the surface yet challenging to maintain, akin to stainless steel appliances free of fingerprints. Living with major depression and anxiety, I recognize the importance of distinguishing this show home facade.

Behind the facade lies a journey that started with empty bank accounts and required relentless effort and sacrifices to progress. What I discuss is the reality: those days when the website and social media look polished, but inwardly, you may feel far from it. Finding balance between appearances and true feelings is a continuous effort for us.

**Return to Play:**
In 2009, I was grappling with severe mental health challenges while maintaining a seemingly perfect exterior—a tenured position, prestigious title, and a home. I traveled globally, discussing disability inclusion and the arts, all while concealing my own disability. My struggle led me to a hospital, where I felt I had reached rock bottom. Yet, unexpectedly, I discovered solace in the hospital's art room. There, I chose the most challenging piece to assert control and prove I was "better." I meticulously controlled every brushstroke, aiming for perfection. However, the outcome was ordinary, not flawless. This disappointment made me realize how much of my life I'd spent chasing perfection. As

a compassionate professional, I always strived to appear dependable and resilient.

It took nearly two weeks before I returned to the art room and gave myself another chance. This time, I chose something spontaneous—a quirky ceramic frog from the shelf. Without overthinking, I randomly splashed it with a hundred different colors. When it emerged from the kiln, I was struck by its beauty. It dawned on me: you can't play in a show home.

**Reminder to self:**
The life of a compassionate professional isn't just about striving **for control and perfection;** it's about embracing imperfection, staying curious, and acknowledging that vulnerability is not a weakness. Many of us hide our struggles to appear strong for others, but this exact act can take a heavy toll on our well-being.

For many, work may not feel like play, but what if I told you it's not about **work versus play**—it's about working "in play." When we discover activities that make us feel brave, creative, connected, and capable, we unlock playful potential in ourselves and others. Countless women have shared with me, "I too battle depression; I'm also a caring professional; I've been through this too, and I've forgotten how to play. Thank you for helping us rediscover it."

Scientifically, when we're afraid, we tend to play less, take fewer risks, and withdraw from connections to protect ourselves. Let's reclaim play in our lives. Play is essential, much like oxygen—we only realize its significance when it's absent.

Let's return to play!

---

**Podcast Episode 389:** Brandi Heather – Return to Play, October 30, 2023
**Contact Information:** https://www.brandiheather.com/

# Diane Wyzga

## Stories From Women Who Walk

*"A woman with a voice is, by definition, a strong woman."*
- Melinda French Gates, American philanthropist

Diane - is the voice behind **"Stories From Women Who Walk,"** a renowned global podcast boasting over 1,100 episodes. Alongside being an RN and JD, Diane serves as the principal story guide and consultant at Quarter Moon Story Arts. Here, she offers personalized coaching to empower women in uncovering their authentic Origin Story—the essence behind their purpose. Witnessing the transformation when women clarify their Origin Story is truly magical. It enables them to confidently articulate their vision, values, and purpose. Now, they are not only seen and heard but understood and listened to as they share ideas, express visions, skillfully negotiate, and influence others powerfully.

**How did it all start in 2019?** A friend suggested, "If you're looking for something to do, you might want to sign up for this podcasting program. It seems right up your alley." Taking their advice felt like drinking from a fire hydrant—intense learning followed one after another. This is how we met. It's been amazing to see how much both our podcasting skills have grown in such a short time. Whether working alone as a storyteller or with guests sharing their stories, consistency and discipline have been crucial.

After a year of interviewing women, I shifted gears to offer my insights in 60 seconds (or a little more!) when I realized I was the only one doing it. Condensing complex concepts, ideas, or messages into such a short time frame was challenging, but I found I excelled at it! Three years later, it continues to impact lives and serves as my audio business card.

I'm thrilled to see where all my listeners are tuning in from. It's incredibly satisfying to watch my listener locations light up on the Simplecast platform. Every day, I make sure to honor my listeners by starting each episode with a shout-out, mentioning their city and state, and including a URL in the episode notes, like Thun, Switzerland. It's my way of expressing gratitude to my global audience.

**How can you create a story in only 60 seconds?** I've learned over time how to distill the heart and essence of a message into a golden nugget that listeners can carry with them throughout their day. My intention is to provide something uplifting, thought-provoking, or inspiring—something that doesn't necessarily require an immediate answer but resonates later as they go about their day.

Each weekday—from Monday through Friday—focuses on a different category or topic. Whatever I create fits into that specific day's theme. For example, those seeking motivation know to tune in on Mondays, while those interested in storytelling find inspiration on Fridays to create their own narratives. My content is guided by what I read, discussions on LinkedIn, current topics, and my personal experiences, helping me sort through ideas and connect with my audience effectively.

Navigating how messages are received can be delicate, and I draw inspiration from the teachings of my teacher, Thich Nhat Hanh:

*"Being mindful when you speak, being mindful when you eat, being mindful when you walk."*

I've found that often, the simplest things have the most profound impact:
- Be present and listen attentively.
- Reflect on the real message and its learning for you.
- Consider what you can take away for today or tomorrow.

My 60 Seconds podcast episodes deliver quick messages or story starters. Once they're out in the airwaves and reach your brainwaves, your imagination takes over, transforming the message into something entirely personal.

I invite you into my space, from Whidbey Island, Washington, to explore what you can create with it in your own imagination and environment.

---

**Podcast Episode 342:** Diane Wyzga – 800 Podcast Episodes with Stories from Women who Walk, January 23, 2024
**Contact Information:**
https://www.quartermoonstoryarts.net/

## What makes a Disruptor?

*"There is a stubbornness about me that can never bear to be frightened at the will of others. My courage always rises at every attempt to intimidate me."*
– Jane Austen, English novelist

Sue lives in Wales. I first met her husband, who was my podcast coach and an amazing support. Sue writes a daily poetic post:

## Listening for the Song of the World (6/22/2023)

Where do you go to listen for the song of the world?
And what do you hear?
Go gently, with hope.
For we are all in this together.

Pause. See differently. Re-Story.

Sue - We live in the hills north of Swansea, just seven or eight miles from the sea. Despite being close, the valley is hidden in the hills, making it very quiet and beautiful here. During the pandemic, it was a privilege to be here because I got to know the valley's little ways, its seasons, and how life works. Not just because we have alpacas, but also because of the wider delights of being in nature.

The interesting thing is that it slows you down—not in the sense of restricting you from doing things, but by helping you move with nature's rhythms and notice more around and within yourself. Walking in the valley is the place to be. It not only provides inspiration for my writing and poetry and the conversations I have with people, but it also helps me breathe more deeply and take in much more. It shifts you from being predominantly in your analytical left brain to engaging your creative right brain. We need that much more.

**Quiet Disruptors:**
I came up with the phrase a few years ago when I needed a quick way to introduce myself, given my unusual background. I don't fit into a box easily. I started out in rural development, worked in universities in education, marketing, and business planning. I've worked with people who are homeless and was later headhunted to work in healthcare. I opened many doors to leading and looking at the healthcare system in innovative ways. The leadership model I introduced in healthcare was a plurality of leadership, which emphasized the need for both clinical leadership, from those who understand medicine, and strategic leadership, working together as peers. Eventually, I took on my first formal job inside the NHS as a Chief Executive Officer.

I quietly challenged the status quo. I'm not someone who stands up on a soapbox, becoming loud and telling people what to do. On the contrary, I believe in inspiring, encouraging, and provoking people so they can become the change they want to see. Hence the phrase "quiet disruptor"—this is me.

I started to write a daily blog, which led to my book **"Quiet Disruptors – Creating Change Without Shouting."** The book identifies the characteristics of quiet disruptors:

- They reframe change through their curiosity, creativity and convictions.
- They provide space for everyone to flourish.

---

**Podcast Episode 380:** Sue Heatherington – Quiet Disruptors, September 4, 2023
**Contact Information:** https://quietdisruptors.com/about/

# Val Lovelace

## Surviving the New Normal

*"Know what sparks the light in you so that you, in your own way, can illuminate the world."*
- Oprah Winfrey, TV personality


Val and I met at Nestlé and have stayed connected through social media. She is the founder and executive director of Maine Death with Dignity and a retired Navy veteran with 20 years of service. Val holds a Master's Degree in Human Relations and a Bachelor's Degree in Industrial Technology. In June 2022, she was ordained as an Interfaith Chaplain after completing a two-year program with the Chaplaincy Institute of Maine. When she's not doing "death stuff," as her son describes it, Val enjoys spending time with her two amazing grandsons and working on various creative projects. She also volunteers on a clergy call-line, providing judgment-free and compassionate spiritual care to people facing decisions and experiences related to pregnancy, parenting, abortion, and adoption. Additionally, Val is an accomplished artist and writer and a wonderful person.

**Asking for Help is Not Easy:** Val - asking for help started for me about four years ago. I woke up one morning with swirly black things in my left eye—it felt like my eye was full of crows or blackbirds. I called my eye doctor, and he calmly told me I needed to see him immediately. It turned out I had a spontaneous injury to my left retina during the night. It's not repairable. I have a condition called pathologic myopia, which puts a lot of stress on the internal parts of the eye because of the shape of my eyeballs. I'm losing my vision in both eyes to this disease. Right after Thanksgiving that year, I had to ask for help because I had to stop driving. I didn't want to cause an accident or hurt someone.

This is where my community comes into play. I'm part of a women's writing group that a friend of mine started here on the island. This group began right when the pandemic hit, and they have become like sisters to me. I also have very dear neighbors and friends in the area who help me get to doctor's appointments, buy groceries, or just get out of the house for a nice breakfast or lunch.

**The New Normal:**
One thing I've been reflecting on is how automated my life used to be. When your eyesight starts failing, you can't rely on that anymore. Recently, there was an incident that taught me to adapt: I had two cartons in my refrigerator, both with a little bit of green on them. One had beef broth, and the other had milk. Without thinking, I reached into the fridge, grabbed what I thought was the milk, and poured it generously onto my oatmeal—it was the beef broth.

I'm very fortunate to have an accessibility specialist from the Veterans Administration who visits once a week. She teaches me helpful tips and tricks. To prevent another oatmeal incident, I now put a rubber band around the milk carton. This way, I can reach into the fridge and feel for the rubber band without relying on color.

Additionally, I'm learning how to **fold money** in my wallet since it's hard for me to see the denominations. The other day, I handed a waitress a hundred-dollar bill, thinking it was a twenty. I'm now using an app that lets me scan a bill with my phone, and it tells me the denomination. Learning how to cope with blindness after being fully sighted is a lot like learning a new language.

**How Can we Help?** This is where having the courage to ask for help comes in. I need to live closer to my family. My son and his family are about an hour and a half away, and as my vision declines, it will be harder for me to live independently. We're building an in-law addition onto his home, so I can live right next door to my lovely grandkids. It's amazing how the community is coming together to help me. I'm not used to being the recipient of this kind of help, but the kindness and generosity from so many people is making this dream possible. This has been a difficult but comforting journey for sure.

You have given so much to others; now it's our time to give back to you and pay it forward.

---

**Podcast Episode 386:** Val Beebe-Lovelace, asking for help is never easy, October 16, 2023
**Contact Information:** https://www.gofundme.com/f/help-val-build-an-accessible-addition
Facebook: @Val Beebe_Lovelace

# Melissa Fisher

## A Business Intrapreneur

*"You are never too small to make a difference."*
- Greta Thunberg, environmental activist

Melissa and I met during the AltMBA program by Akimbo amidst the pandemic in March 2020, a time when the future looked uncertain. Despite never meeting face-to-face, I value the virtual support we provide each other.

Melissa - lives on Kauai, describes herself as a people person. She enjoys connecting with others while traveling, working, or simply strolling down the street. She's passionate about solving business challenges and excels at bringing project pieces together into a cohesive whole. Melissa is deeply curious about people, technology, learning, and enhancing everyday creativity.

**The Carbon Almanac:**
The Carbon Almanac has been a delightful project to collaborate on with individuals spanning various time zones and corners of the globe. Thanks to technology, both the AltMBA and the Carbon Almanac have enabled me to engage with kindred spirits regardless of my geographical location. Although I wasn't involved in writing the almanac itself, I joined a team later on to translate its information into actionable steps, a process we call:

"Connecting the Carbon Dots."
(https://connectthecarbondots.com/).

It's about making connections to navigate through the daily flood of information, which can feel overwhelming. Questions like "What's next?" and "What can I do now?" or even deeper queries like:

- How can I make a difference?
- How can I enact change?

These questions formed the foundation for our team to bridge information with actionable steps, highlighting broader connections. We explore how these actions influence the carbon cycle and emissions. The most impactful step you can take is advocacy—raising your voice to drive change. It begins with understanding and making conscious choices, finding your community, and uniting with like-minded individuals. Together, we can implement these changes and create a meaningful impact.

Throughout our conversations since 2020, Melissa has expressed her aspiration to be an entrepreneur. However, considering her current role, she embodies more of an intrapreneurial spirit. An intrapreneur operates within an organization but approaches her work with an entrepreneurial mindset.

There are many things we have in common, but some are also different:

| Intrapreneur – Melissa | Entrepreneur - Susanne |
| --- | --- |
| Clients | Clients |
| Colleagues / Team | No Team |
| Routine | Glamorous working globally |
| Routine | Freedom |
| 9-5+ job | 24/7 job |
| Managing ateam & projects | Manage clients and projects |
| Having one boss | Having multiple bosses as your clients are your boss |
| Motivating self and teams | Motivating SELF and others without any control, i.e., influencing without authority |
| Delegation of tasks beyond scope of role | Me, myself, and I are doing all the work |
| Steady paycheck | Work on projects / invoice when completed |
| 20 + Vacation days | … 😊 not sure, dreaming of a vacation. |
| Every other Friday off | My clients dictate my calendar. |

There are always trade-offs in every role. Be curious, help others and enjoy what you do.

*"The grass is always greener on the other side."*

---

**Podcast Episode 382:** Melissa SP Fisher – Intrapreneur vs. Entrepreneur? September 18, 2023
**Contact Information:**
https://www.linkedin.com/in/melissaspfisher/

# Jennifer Ashford

## Rebirth beyond FIRE!

*"Where there is love and inspiration,
I don't think you can go wrong."*
- Ella Fitzgerald, jazz singer


Jennifer, a special guest for our 400th episode, shares her life stories of overcoming tough times with mindfulness and a focus on helping others.

I met Jennifer in 2018. She holds a Bachelor's Degree in Early Childhood Education and a Master's Degree in Educational Leadership. Throughout her career, she has taught kindergarten and raised three children. Our paths crossed during a mindfulness training session.

**Her background:**
Jennifer - I work at a Chicago public school. I began my journey in pre-K and now I teach kindergarten. I initially thought pre-K was my calling because I've always wanted to be a catalyst for change. It's incredibly fulfilling to start with young children, shaping and imparting foundational skills to them.

Over time, I moved to teaching kindergarteners how to read, and later I transitioned to first grade. Each step has been a learning process not just for my students, but for me as well.

As an educator, I thrive on learning and I'm still exploring my path forward.

I advocate first and foremost because of my extensive experience in this field. My passion lies in understanding the specific needs of children, particularly in urban communities. Teaching children of color presents unique challenges—they often face issues like trauma, food insecurity, and community violence. A hungry mind cannot learn, and a mind affected by trauma struggles even more.

**The house is on fire:**
I'm known in my family as the caretaker, always looking out for everyone. Lately, I've faced the challenge of not having a stable home anymore. A couple of years ago, my grandmother passed away, and then my uncle moved in with me. After that, my partner and I decided to live together. In July 2023, we experienced an electrical fire that woke us all up at 6 AM. The dog's barking and someone yelling "FIRE!" alerted us to the danger.

When we woke up, the back room of the house was engulfed in flames and thick smoke, resembling a forest fire. Knowing the danger of inhaling such dense smoke, I knew not to attempt to enter. While most people don't perish directly from fire, the inhalation of smoke can be fatal.

I started yelling and calling for my children immediately. My uncle, who was in the enclosed back porch area, was disoriented and fell, yet he bravely ventured into the flames to search for everyone and ensure they got out safely.

Standing outside, we didn't have time to think about shoes or clothes; we were in our pajamas. It was 6 AM, still dark and rainy. Fortunately, the fire hadn't spread to the front of the house yet, so I dashed back inside to grab my car keys and phone.

After calling 911, the fire grew louder with breaking glass. We stood there, barefoot and some of us shirtless, when neighbors rushed to cover us with coats, provided shoes, and shielded us with umbrellas. They came out, asking if we were okay and offering their homes for shelter.

Where's my dog? I heard him barking, but he never came out with us. As the firefighters searched, I suddenly realized I hadn't heard him bark anymore. Finally, they found him and performed CPR to revive him. In that moment, everything stopped for me. Tears streamed down my face as I felt immense gratitude—everyone was safely out of the house, and seeing my dog revived was a moment of renewal for all of us.

This experience is shaping me in ways I never expected. After the fire, we stayed with a relative for about two weeks, and my sister started a GoFundMe page, which was a difficult but necessary step for us. Later, we found refuge at a family friend's home. Throughout it all, I'm learning to find the rainbow after the storm, to see the silver linings and lessons in adversity.

**Now what? How did you get through this?**
That sense of rebirth came from feeling like I had to start over again and again. The shock aftermath felt so real. We needed everything—sheets, pillows, pillowcases, cookware, and personal hygiene items. It made us realize how much we take for granted until it's suddenly gone.

As a mother of three, caring for my grown children, our dog, and managing the household while dealing with school starting again requires strength drawn from life's experiences. With age comes wisdom and learning, and it was through the TeamUp mindfulness training that I met Susanne, Jeanne, and Ranga—fellow learners who became important in my life.

In 2018, I felt like a hurricane, ready to storm away due to the weight I was carrying inside. It was like having a wound that wouldn't heal, despite repeatedly applying Band-Aids. I realized I needed to accept things as they are, without trying to change what was happening. After the fire, I embraced acceptance and believed that something better would come for my family and me. I'm grateful that we all made it out alive, without any injuries or fatalities. Seeing my dog return was a symbol of hope and renewal for us all.

**What is your wish for this year?**
My goal for this year is to secure a permanent home for us. While we're grateful to stay at a friend's house, it doesn't feel like our own sanctuary. Our new place will be our haven of peace. My son recently commented on our current situation, saying, "We only have one outlet in my room, and I don't

like that." He didn't ask for anything for Christmas, but he's looking forward to having his own room in our new home, where he can plug in multiple devices for his TV and computer.

**Gratitude**: Our entire family came together to create a video celebrating the 400th episode of "Take it from the Ironwoman."

---

**Podcast Episode 400:** Jennifer Ashford - Celebration of Life, January 15, 2024
**Contact** **Information:**
https://www.gofundme.com/f/9ww3r-help-our-family
Facebook: @Jennifer Ashford

# LEADING

*"The true power comes from standing in your own truth and walking your own path."*
– Elizabeth Gilbert, writer

Leadership is often invisible yet impactful—a testament to life lessons and stories. We are all leaders of our own lives; whether driving or taking a train, we choose our direction. Rarely do we wander aimlessly without a destination in mind.

**What defines leaders? How can I become one?**
Leaders are those who go the extra step, taking that additional mile few are willing to travel. It's about giving that extra 2%, no matter the challenges.

We can draw inspiration not only from celebrity leaders but also from those who quietly do incredible work behind the scenes. To truly elevate lipstick leadership, we need to introspect, fostering self-awareness and mindfulness. Take the opportunity to absorb the lessons from these stories.

**Learning, listening, and leading** are intertwined on the path to becoming the leader you aspire to be.

# Doina Fischer

## A unique Pair: Horses and Leadership

*"Never forget to dream."*
– Madonna, singer

Doina is a remarkable person whom I met years ago in New York City; we are both from Switzerland. I occasionally assisted Doina with mundane office tasks, through which I gained insights from her equestrian background. It was a unique learning experience for me. Always stay open to learning something new!

Doina - now lives in Costa del Sol, Spain, where she leads her business, **Classical Riding Reflection.** She specializes in training horses and providing equestrian lessons. Doina also helps clients find horses and offers boarding services. She travels extensively to conduct equestrian clinics worldwide and occasionally judges equestrian competitions.

As part of a new program, Doina allows anyone to ride her well-trained horse to experience what it's like to ride a trained horse. Clients visiting Spain can enjoy the Spanish lifestyle, staying in beautiful apartments and spending leisure time by the pool. It's a fantastic combination: riding lessons in the morning, relaxing by the pool in the afternoon, and returning to the farm for more riding later in the day. Viva España!

**Your business: Classical Riding Reflection**
With **Classical Riding Reflection**, I offer coaching sessions that parallel what someone might do as a business or life coach with people. Additionally, I specialize in dressage, which is akin to the art of performing gymnastics in a competition—it's the dance of horse and rider in harmony. I also work with horses dealing with physical issues, focusing on their strength and overall health. Teaching riders and fostering a deep connection between them and their horses, while also delving into biomechanics, brings me immense joy and fulfillment.

**Teaching in New York, Florida, Brazil, and Spain:**
I taught horseback riding in New York City for many years. Some people might not realize that there was a riding school, one of the oldest in the United States, near Central Park called Claremont. I worked there for six years until it closed down. After New York, I moved to Florida, where most of the equestrian competitions take place. Each winter, I brought horses to Florida for my clients to compete because it's too cold in the northern US. Following my time in Florida, I spent seven years in Brazil working with breeders of Lusitano horses, which are originally from Portugal. Brazilians are the largest breeders of Lusitanos in the world. After Brazil, I returned to Europe and now live on the Costa del Sol in Spain, working in a professional stable with jumpers from all over Europe.

**Being innovative and a disruptor:**
During the pandemic, life didn't stop for me because the horses still needed feeding and training. To continue

teaching my riders, I discovered how useful apps like WhatsApp can be for video and voice calls. I would have someone film the rider while I coached them through a voice call, which was a challenge because the filmer had to stay focused for about 45 minutes. Now, other apps have made this process much smoother. In tough times, being innovative and breaking from tradition is crucial.

Recently, I used this virtual method to teach a woman in Texas. She was thrilled with the lesson and sent me a message saying it was the best she'd had in months. Many clients have benefited from virtual classes and shown significant improvement. Thankfully, in-person clinics are now starting up again as the world opens up.

**Fast forward:**
Doina has developed a new course that's open to everyone, even those who aren't familiar with horses: "Equine Reflection on Human Emotions."

---

**Podcast Episode 82:** Doina Fischer – Online Horse Training with Classical Riding Reflections - Costa del Sol, Spain, September 5, 2020
**Contact Information:** https://classicalridingreflection.com/

## The Samanta S. Ribary Foundation supporting Orphans and Children in Need

*"Many strange things happen in this world."*
– Johanna Spyri, Swiss author

Evelyne Ribary - I was born and raised in Switzerland. Then I immigrated to the United States together with my husband, Urs. I was working as a supervisor in medical laboratory technology in clinical and research at Rockefeller University in New York. Evelyne and I met through our mutual friend Yvonne Condrau.

When my husband, Urs, and I decided to start a family, we adopted an orphaned child from South America. We traveled to Ecuador to meet our daughter, Samanta, who had been abandoned by her biological parents and found at a local marketplace when she was just two months old. After eight months of intensive searching for her biological family, the court confirmed that she was abandoned and eligible for international adoption. Samanta quickly bonded with us, and we spent three weeks together in Ecuador finalizing her adoption process.

During that time, we realized how challenging it must be for other orphans, especially older children with disabilities, whether physical or mental, to find a permanent home. We strongly felt the need to do more than just spend time at the orphanage. That's when we decided to establish a charity in our daughter's honor. Our goal is to support orphans, ensuring they grow up in safe, nurturing environments where their physical, intellectual, emotional, and social needs are met daily. Research indicates that early childhood is crucial for a child's development and learning abilities.

Our goal was to provide essential support such as medication, food, and clothing, while also enhancing local facilities and childcare services. Additionally, we aimed to offer educational opportunities through learning programs for older orphans. We worked to improve existing infrastructure and supported single mothers to help them keep their children within their biological families, thereby preventing children from becoming orphans.

**Success stories:**
- Two young men, formerly orphans themselves, installed a playground sponsored by the Samanta S. Ribary Foundation (SSRF) as a way of giving back to the orphanage in Ecuador where they grew up.
- In collaboration with SOS Children's Villages, our second project was to build daycare centers in four cities across Ecuador, providing care for newborns to six-year-old children.
- The Samanta S. Ribary Foundation (SSRF) also partnered to rebuild orphanages and schools in Pakistan following a devastating earthquake.

Inspired by the foundation's journey and our daughter's story, we authored a children's book titled **"Samanta's**

**Journey of Hope."** Originally written and published in German as "Samanta und die blaue Blume," it was later translated into English. The book features colorful illustrations and is based on our daughter's real-life experiences.

**A paragraph from the book:**

"Samanta asked the blue flower, 'Where am I going? Why is this woman carrying me on her back? Where do I belong? Where is my home?' The blue flower reassured her, 'Don't worry, Samanta, my child, you are safe. You're beginning your journey of hope.' Above the clouds, the paradise bird soared, guiding them through the mountains. Samanta couldn't take her eyes off the paradise bird. She recognized it among the other birds, knowing it was there, watching over her, eager to share more with her."

Today, Samanta is a young woman who has become a successful equestrian show jumper and Grand Prix rider. After graduating with honors from high school, she began her studies at Simon Fraser University in Vancouver, Canada. Samanta is highly motivated and deeply dedicated, with a passion for caring for animals.

---

**Podcast Episode 307:** Evelyne Ribary – Samanta S. Ribary Foundation, June 6, 2022

**Contact Information:** https://www.samanta-ribary-foundation.org

# Janet Groom & Caroline Palmy

**Heart and Soul**

*"Do what you feel in your heart to be right –
for you'll be criticized anyway."*
- Eleanor Roosevelt, former First Lady of the United States

Janet and I first met in 2005 at Nestlé. I advocated for her to be hired by her manager. Later, she relocated to Switzerland, where she connected with Caroline. In 2017, Janet organized a Body, Mind, and Soul event in Zürich, Switzerland where we both spoke.

Today, Janet and Caroline co-host **"Heart and Soul,"** a weekly video podcast that has been running successfully for over a year.

Caroline resides in Switzerland and works as a heart flow healer. Her passion lies in assisting women in reconnecting with their hearts, combating feelings of inadequacy and unworthiness. Caroline believes that if everyone could embrace their inherent worth and greatness, it would significantly improve the world.

Her work focuses on empowering women to cultivate self-love, which forms the core of the "Heart and Soul" podcast.

Janet identifies herself as the "soul" of the team. With a background in coaching that has shifted focus since moving from Switzerland back to the UK, she acknowledges the challenging transition and credits Caroline for helping her realign with her purpose and rediscover self-love. Janet's current work leans towards the spiritual aspects of life coaching and NLP (neuro-linguistic programming). In her discussions today, she explores energy systems and their connection to the soul, emphasizing how individuals can tap into their soul for guidance.

**Misconception Introverts vs. Extroverts:**
"In one of their episodes, they discuss introverts versus extroverts. I've been curious about this topic for a while and would love to hear insights from experts."

**Susanne** shared, "It's funny that everyone thinks I'm a total extrovert. But the more I think about it, I'm not that much of an extrovert. I really cherish my alone time—that's why I love running. Maybe I'm more of an introvert?"

**Caroline and Janet** find it fascinating because there are many misconceptions about introverts. Both of them are introverts themselves, but they're just regular people. They enjoy being around others and going to parties.

The distinction between introverts and extroverts lies in how they recharge. Extroverts recharge their energy by being around others—they thrive on social interaction and feel energized and validated in social settings. On the other hand, introverts tend to recharge in solitude. They prefer less social interaction and find renewal and energy in quiet, solitary activities.

**Caroline** shared, "Parties are fine, but after two to three hours, I start feeling tired and drained. People often think introverts are loners who can't socialize, but that's not true. We just need more time to recharge on our own. I cherish spending time alone in nature—it really helps me recharge my batteries."

**Janet** shared, "For me, it was about masking, especially as women, we've become quite adept at it. That's why people might see us as extroverts. But it's a learned adaptation. The challenge with masking is that it's incredibly draining and exhausting—it's hard work. As you get older, your tolerance for constant socializing decreases. Maybe when you're younger, you have more energy and tolerance for being around people rather than being alone."

**Fast forward:**
Their weekly podcast and video series have also been adapted into books! Follow them as they explore everyday topics that resonate deeply with many listeners.

---

**Podcast Episode 384:** Caroline Palmy and Janet Groom – Heart and Soul, October 2, 2023
**Contact Information:**
Caroline Palmy: https://carolinepalmy.com/
Janet Groom: https://janetgroom.com/

# Sushi Yogi

## Body, Mind and Spiritual Wellness

*"Yoga is the art and science of living."*
– Indra Devi, lovingly referred to as the first lady of yoga

Sushmitha Shrikant "Sushi Yogi" is a yoga coach and wellness mentor with over ten years of dedicated study and extensive training totaling seven hundred hours. I had the pleasure of meeting her in India while visiting her family in Chennai.

**Why the name Sushi?**
I chose it because I wanted a name that rhymed, like "Sushi" and "Yogi." It's been my nickname for quite some time now.

**What do you do?**
Sushi - I'm a yoga teacher, entrepreneur, traveler, and student. A large part of me is still discovering the way in which I can share my yoga with the world, so it doesn't feel too much like pop yoga. There aren't many South Indian voices in the yoga world, so I'm trying to carve out a unique space. My yoga style is based on ancient techniques that date back 5,000 years. I aim to adapt these practices for people who only have 10 to 15 minutes in the morning to calm their nerves and center themselves before starting their day.

I don't just see myself as a yoga teacher anymore. I've come to understand that teaching yoga goes beyond showing a sequence. It's about integrating yoga philosophy and helping people discover more about themselves. I'm gradually moving towards being a spiritual guide in this field. It's about creating an energy that inspires change and encourages people to focus on 'being' rather than constant busyness and doing.

**How do you pay your bills?**
Good question: How can I keep this genuine? This is a real service I want to provide. I want it to be affordable for everyone without cheapening its true essence. The yoga teaching field is crowded. In India, people charge less than a dollar a month for classes because they have so many students. It's hard to compete with that.

What I have seen, we're moving towards luxury wellness retreats at top-tier hotels. It's becoming an exclusive experience for those who can afford it. For instance, a two-night retreat can easily cost a couple of thousand dollars at a luxury resort. These represent the two extremes in the market.
What I've found is that there will always be people who deeply appreciate and benefit from authentic yoga. There will never be a shortage of those who value yoga. This belief gives me confidence that yoga's significance will endure over the long term. I'm dedicated to sharing the true value of yoga with others.

**Travels:**
A few years ago, I discovered Yoga Trade (yogatrade.com), a platform for yoga teachers to exchange work. I was drawn

to an organization called 'Yoga for Wellness Africa' in Tanzania, where they supported both for-profit and NGO initiatives. I admired their model because I wanted to give back while sustaining myself. Traveling solo to Tanzania, I taught mindfulness to children despite the language barrier.

Later, I taught yoga in luxurious resorts with pools. These experiences immersed me in diverse settings, where I found a common thread: yoga's universal usefulness transcends language barriers. Whether with local communities or luxury settings, I realized yoga's power lies in its embodiment—a sacred practice that surpasses words and linguistic imperfections.

---

**Podcast Episode 326:** Sushmita Shrikanth – Sushi Yogi, A Global Yoga Coach, October 10, 2022
**Contact Information:** Instagram: @sushi.yogi | Sushmitha | Ashtanga Yoga Teacher

# Dinah Salonga

## Coaching Leaders more Wisdom

*"Just because you are CEO, don't think you have landed.
You must continually increase your learning, the way you
think, and the way you approach the organization."*
- Indra Nooyi, former chairperson, CEO of PepsiCo


Dinah - during the pandemic, I moved to the northern Philippines to join a community focused on spiritual growth. Since then, I've gained a deeper sense of enlightenment, especially in my work with leaders. Dinah and I met through the Asian Leadership Institute, where we both serve as mindfulness facilitators and coaches.

**What do you do now?**
I am a leadership mentor at the **Wisdom Institute for Leadership and Global Advancement,** where we strive to inspire wisdom in leaders and conscience in entrepreneurs. Today, we see a lot of greed driven by profit. By fostering wisdom and conscience in our leaders and businesspeople, they can improve not only their own earnings but also benefit their consumers, stakeholders, and the environment.

At the Institute, I focus on the **self-development pillar.** We have three pillars: **self-care, self-development, and self-mastery.** Under the self-development pillar, our main program is the Balanced-Life Strategy Program, which helps successful leaders find balance in the five key areas of life.

In corporations, we often talk about work-life balance, but this only covers two aspects.

Many leaders neglect their health in pursuit of money and success. Another aspect is social contribution, where we give back to society not just through charity, but by offering our time, talent, and resources to help humanity. Finally, there's spiritual life, which many people overlook. This involves finding our higher purpose and mission in life.

Why are you here? This is about who you are, not what you are. We often introduce ourselves with titles and achievements: "I am the CEO of this," or "I have won this award." But these are just what you do. Who you are as a person is much more important to discover. That is spirituality—discovering your true essence.

As leaders, we always aim to improve, and this journey is a path to enlightenment. We continually learn, grow, and strive for personal development.

Another aspect we need to balance as leaders is our trinity of success: intelligence, love, and willpower. All leaders are intelligent; that's why they become leaders. However, there's often an imbalance in love and willpower. Leaders who are loving may have less willpower, and those with strong willpower may show less love.

Our programs help you **develop the aspects of your leadership style** that are weaker. If you have less willpower, we offer workshops to strengthen it. Some leaders are very loving but lack willpower. To balance this, you can engage in dynamic activities like martial arts or boxing, which build strong energy and willpower. Loving leaders often prefer activities like yoga, which match their personalities. To balance this, they need more dynamic activities to develop their fire and will.

Conversely, leaders with strong willpower and energy often dislike yoga, finding it too slow. They need practices that are contemplative and meditative, which expand their heart, or they can engage in more service-oriented activities.

Balancing this trinity of intelligence, love, and willpower leads to greater success and enlightenment as a leader.

---

**Podcast Episode 394:** Dinah Salonga – Balanced Life Strategist, Philippines, November 27, 2023
**Contact Information:** https://www.wilgaglobal.com/
https://www.linkedin.com/in/dinah-salonga

# Janin Ricalde

## Women Leadership and Beyond

*"Leadership is about making others better as a result of your presence, and, making sure that impact lasts in your absence."*
- Sheryl Sandberg, former COO, Facebook

Janin invited me to be a part of her Women Leadership and Beyond Conference in 2021.

Janin - I live in Merida, in the Yucatan Peninsula, Mexico. I am a woman in the business world, having worked in business since I was very young. I believe that great and successful organizations are those where employees and companies are committed to each other as equals, regardless of gender. I have a Master's Degree in Human Resources and a Bachelor's Degree in Business Administration. I have been researching and studying competencies and leadership in this field for a long time. I love this area because it allows me to develop and support people in building their skills and knowledge. Despite my extensive experience in human resources, I still feel like a seventeen-year-old with many ideas on how we can make things even better today.

I always have many projects I'm working on. One that is very dear to my heart is building my own consulting firm in Merida, Mexico, focusing on **"Women Leadership and Beyond,"** which supports women from around the world.

Our vision is to help women build their skills for both professional and personal goals. Many ask how we can achieve this, and I believe the first ingredient is a strong will. It's the will to get things done and make good decisions. As women, we need to break paradigms and stereotypes.

On March 9 and 10, 2021, we organized a successful summit for **Women Leadership and Beyond**.

**What was the pivotal moment to let's do this?**
I am a teacher at the State University here in Merida. A few summers ago, I taught a fabulous, motivated group of female students who needed to create an international event or summit for their final Master's project. I was enthusiastic about this venture and had a vision: "Let's make it happen." I started connecting with colleagues who might say YES, including you.

Initially, it started as a school project, but we soon realized it had potential beyond being just an academic endeavor. It grew into something much bigger and more impactful. I felt deeply honored to be a part of it as I witnessed everyone's contributions and the success we achieved together. We even had someone dedicate a song to us—it felt like we were celebrities.

I empowered the team from behind the scenes, and I saw everyone stepping up. When you empower others, they are motivated to showcase their best and most creative work. This happened naturally for us. We worked tirelessly, many long days together, showing that sisterhood is key to our success. It's how we break through ideas, stereotypes, and beyond—hence the name **"Women Leadership and Beyond"** (WLB). Everyone had a voice. I provided some initial ideas, and the students demonstrated their creativity to bring them to life. I am truly happy.

Merida in the Yucatan Peninsula is smaller compared to Mexico City, Guadalajara, or Monterrey. While known for tourism, the area has been evolving into a more industrial and innovative part of the country. I'm delighted to see this positive change beyond tourism.

The conference spanned over two magical days where sharing and caring were fully evident. I hope there will be a way to continue from where we left off. The event was conducted in both English and Spanish, making it a truly global gathering, and it sparked a global movement after those magical days.

My dream is to contribute to creating a better world for women in every field. Good luck, Janin – we're with you for your next venture!

---

**Podcast Episode 147:** Janin Ricalde - Women Leadership and Beyond - Merida, Mexico, January 27, 2021
**Contact Information:** Facebook: @WMENLB – Women Leadership and Beyond

## Bridging Worlds as an Interpreter and Translator

*"At the end of the day,
we can endure much more than we think we can."*
- Frida Kahlo, Mexican painter, and activist

Lucy - CEO of **Translation 4 All**, a small agency offering interpretation and translation services in all languages, including various dialects. I became a certified interpreter at UCLA and in the State of California. While I've had the privilege of interpreting for Presidents, heads of state, and other prominent figures, what really fulfilled me was seeing how our services helped people from diverse backgrounds grasp concepts that were unfamiliar to them but common knowledge to others. For us, this embodies the true meaning of "knowledge is power."

Early in my career, my goal was to interpret for the United Nations in Geneva on a rotational basis, six months on and six months off. However, when I became pregnant, I realized this lifestyle wouldn't work for my young family. Instead, I focused on local interpreting jobs and began building my client base. It was my husband who suggested we start our own agency, which we did successfully. We handled criminal interpretations and worked extensively with school districts.

My involvement with mental health began when I started interpreting expulsion hearings. I vividly remember a case involving two children, aged 12 and 11, who brought a switchblade to school after being bullied. They faced expulsion, and I noticed similar incidents occurring weekly, with expelled students often transferring their problems to new schools. It became clear that something crucial was missing in supporting these children—beyond just language interpretation.

I realized these kids needed more than just translation services; they needed therapy and support from professionals. This realization marked a shift from interpreting for high-profile clients to advocating for vulnerable students in Los Angeles. Through this work, I aimed to reduce the expulsion rates among non-native speakers and provide comprehensive care to those in need.

**Working with the stars:** Everyone's interested in celebrities, especially being close to Hollywood, California. I can share a story about the OJ Simpson case. The interpreter for the nanny who testified live on television wasn't doing a good job. That evening, I went on a popular Los Angeles channel and highlighted the significant discrepancies between what the nanny said and how the interpreter was translating it. Shortly afterward, the interpreter for Judge Ito was replaced. It was important to me to ensure the truth about what happened was known.
One of my favorite celebrity stories involves being in the right place at the right time—when preparation meets opportunity. My father, a boxing enthusiast, took me to

Caesar's Palace in Las Vegas one evening to watch Oscar de la Hoya fight. After the match, the trainer, who was from Mexico, came out to address the audience and the media. They asked if anyone bilingual was in the crowd, and this was my moment. Encouraged by my family, I stepped up and interpreted for him.

It was intimidating with all the cameras around, knowing my words would be heard worldwide. But it was also a tremendous honor to showcase my skills while sitting next to Oscar himself, his manager, and others. This experience marked the beginning of my journey.

Years later, I found myself interpreting at a mental health symposium, which sparked my interest in the field. I started seeking more opportunities in this area, attending summits and conferences that provided me with valuable insights. However, I noticed a significant gap: despite the strides being made by experts in mental health, the information about available resources wasn't reaching everyday people like you and me. Even employers and academic institutions seemed unaware of these crucial services.

Mental health deserves attention across various sectors, not just academia. The pandemic highlighted a significant issue in our personal lives that urgently needed addressing. We saw a rise in suicides, increased prescriptions for antidepressants, anti-anxiety, and anti-insomnia medications—many for first-time users. This underscores the serious challenges many faced without seeking help.

It's crucial to openly discuss mental health to break down the stigma, allowing people to feel free to talk about their struggles and support others in need.

Lucy also participated in the **Women Leadership and Beyond** summit, interpreting for the entire two days and highlighting the importance of mental health. This summit is just one step; we must continue supporting each other and raising awareness.

---

**Podcast Episode 147:** Lucy Ferraez Rivero - Women Leadership and Beyond – Mental Health, February 11, 2021
**Contact Information:** https://translation4all.com/

# Virginie Glaenzer

## Challenging the Status Quo for the Future

*"The world is starving for new ideas and
great leaders who will champion those ideas."*
– Lisa Su, first woman to lead global tech company
Advanced Micro Devises

Virginie and I first connected at a fundraiser for the "White Roof Project" in New York, where she bid on my coaching sessions. Today, I proudly serve as the Chief Leadership Coach Officer in her organization.

Virginie - is a true trailblazer. Not only is she a successful entrepreneur and leader, but she is also the visionary founder of **AcornOak**, a unique community dedicated to promoting female leadership in fractional roles.

In 2023, she solidified her influence with the publication of **"The Abundance Economy"** and hosts the podcast **Pass the Mic.**

In her role as a fractional Chief Marketing Officer (CMO), Virginie is always on the lookout for emerging trends and isn't afraid to challenge conventional wisdom. Her career began in sales, where she honed her skills in overcoming obstacles; her tenacity in finding solutions, even in the face of adversity, has been a hallmark of her success.

**What's this "Fractional Executive" business all about?**
The concept of fractional executives gained popularity during the pandemic as companies recognized the advantages of having experienced leaders on their team without the full-time commitment.

For example, a fractional CMO devotes a portion of their time and expertise to an organization. This practice extends beyond marketing to fields such as technology, strategy, human resources, and leadership coaching. It allows businesses to benefit from specialized skills and insights while optimizing resources more effectively.

The fractional model stands apart from traditional consulting or project-based freelancing by combining commitment with flexibility. It enables organizations to leverage the expertise of seasoned executives without bearing the full-time salary burden.

This approach promotes innovative work methods and creates substantial opportunities for women in leadership. It fosters a workplace environment that minimizes office politics and guarantees consistent participation in decision-making. This aligns seamlessly with lifestyles that prioritize balance and well-being, making it a compelling choice for both professionals and organizations seeking sustainable growth.

At AcornOak, Virginie takes a hands-on approach by personally curating biographical pages for new members. These pages offer a vibrant alternative to traditional professional profiles found on platforms like LinkedIn. She encourages members to regularly update their stories, emphasizing personal and professional growth. This includes acquiring new skills, discarding outdated ones, and cultivating a culture of continuous evolution and self-improvement within the community.

When not working, Virginie cherishes creating and co-creating, whether it's with a business, through writing, or just while walking her dog. Living in Washington, D.C., she often mixes work with pleasure, whether it's typing away in a museum coffee area or soaking up the city's vibrant art scene.

---

**Podcast Episode 395:** Virginie Glaenzer - Fractional CMO, Executive Advisor Washington, December 11, 2023
**Contact Information:** https://www.acornoak.net/

# Dr. Susanne Cappendijk | "Dr. C"

## Uniting Hands for a Better World

*"Fight for the things that you care about but do it in a way that will lead others to join you."* – Ruth Bader Ginsburg, American lawyer, and Supreme Court Justice

Susanne - ("Dr. C") the founder and CEO of **EDsnaps**—an accomplished neuroscientist, MBA holder, and above all, a compassionate individual who positively impacts many lives through her generous and forward-thinking educational and leadership programs. We crossed paths at a networking event and discovered our shared first name and European background, both speaking English with a charming accent.

EDsnaps is a non-profit organization dedicated to empowering underprivileged female-identifying students by fostering their interest and careers in STEM (science, technology, engineering, math), aiming to turn STEM learners into leaders. They integrate art with STEM and STEM with art, recognizing the creative synergy between disciplines.

In 2020, faced with the challenges of the pandemic, EDsnaps swiftly transitioned all their programs to virtual platforms, adapting their vision for the future into immediate reality. Despite financial hardships and funding delays, they persevered to continue their in-person summer program.

Though funding constraints necessitated adjustments, such as using the New York City subway instead of planned buses for field trips, the organization managed to sustain operations with support from nineteen generous private donors. This ensured essential resources for counselors and student activities, demonstrating EDsnaps' resilience and commitment to their mission amidst adversity.

**How can we become like Dr. C? What's your secret?**
I enjoy seeing wonderful and curious students, but they don't have to be exact replicas of me. However, they should aim for:

- Kindness,
- Positive thinking,
- Openness to new things and a willingness to learn,
- A mindset geared towards becoming tomorrow's leaders.

**EDsnaps program offerings:**
**Food Drive Update**: In 2023, we organized a food drive to support 150 families in the Bronx. We chose February for this initiative instead of traditional holidays like Thanksgiving, when many others host similar events. Our goal is to provide assistance when it's most needed— February, when many families struggle with financial challenges and food shortages, especially during the lingering cold weather.

154

**Promoting Healthy Habits:** We empower students by demonstrating how to grow their own vegetables, integrating this practice with various STEM disciplines such as medicine, physics, and chemistry. Additionally, we enrich the STE(A)M experience by incorporating calligraphy, drawings, and poetry to foster creativity and holistic learning. Our approach encourages students to explore diverse fields while cultivating a healthy lifestyle.

**Exploring Our Garden:** As we tend to our plants, we engage our senses—what do we smell, see, observe, and hear?

**Global Reach:** In 2023, we expanded our impactful Global Youth Leadership Program to Kenya, building on its success in Ghana through virtual platforms.

**Everyday Essential Skills:** We focus on teaching **financial management** and **comprehensive reading,** emphasizing the importance of understanding numbers and the meanings of words. Our programs are conducted in a safe and enjoyable environment, with live sessions where everyone is welcome as they are—no recordings.

**Leadership Principles:** Our counselors and students are amazing—they watch out for each other. No one gets left behind, except when they're late for a field trip! Sometimes, we have to enforce rules strictly. Students know they can be dismissed from the program if necessary. I believe in second chances, but if someone squanders theirs, they understand they're out. There's much work ahead, and I hope people understand that by working together, we can serve more communities and create a better world for everyone.

Thank you so much for everything you do for everyone. We're here to support you on your journey through many more summer programs with EDsnaps, using our EDsnapian mindset.

**Fast forward:**
In 2023, students and counselors in our Summer Program "All STEAM Stars" had an unforgettable experience visiting a 777 long-range wide-body airliner at JFK Airport in New York City. Students enjoyed lunch in business class, discovering firsthand that the sky is not the limit.

In 2024, EDsnaps remains committed to providing high-quality education. Access to quality education empowers STEM learners to become STEM leaders. Our programs focus on helping students recognize their own brain power, boosting their self-esteem.

Our 2024 theme, "All STEM Gems," emphasizes that harnessing your brain power is key to personal and professional success.

---

**Podcast Episode 333:** EDsnaps - Look at all the successes in 2022, Dr. C, November 21, 2022
**Contact Information:** https://www.edsnaps.org/

# Sam Payne

## The Strength of The Pink Elephants Network

*"Being human, we are imperfect. That's why we need each other. To catch each other when we falter. To encourage each other when we lose heart. Some may lead; others may follow; but none of us can go it alone."*
– Hilary Clinton, former First Lady of the United States

Sam is the CEO and founder of The Pink Elephants Support Network, a charity that supports people affected by early pregnancy loss or miscarriage. I met Sam through Melissa, an intrapreneur from the AltMBA program.

**The topic that is a taboo:** For a long time, early pregnancy loss and miscarriage have been topics rarely discussed. Globally, there's a lack of awareness and empathy for the experiences of many mothers and partners. Additionally, there are not enough clear policies to support people during this difficult time.

Sam - I have personally experienced pregnancy loss, specifically recurrent pregnancy loss. We struggled to have our second child and had two miscarriages in a row. After my second miscarriage, I realized there was a significant gap in support and understanding.

"I'm asking for support, saying, 'I'm not coping.
I don't know how to get through this alone.'

I said it to health professionals, friends, and colleagues, but I was met with awkward silences. They didn't know how to respond and might have thought I was slightly crazy. No one offered to help. Then I found another woman, Gaby, who had her own journey with IVF and miscarriages. She was the first person who truly understood what I was going through. I was enormously grateful to finally connect with someone who understood, allowing me to be honest without having to put on a brave face. This connection, based on shared experience, was instrumental in building the Pink Elephants Support Network eight years ago.

**What is the right approach to help? What can we say?**

*"I'm sorry for your loss. I'm here for you.
What can I do for you?"*

This could mean sending flowers, just as you would for any other type of loss. It could involve looking after their older children, giving them space to grieve without having to put on a brave face. Practical support can make a big difference. Even a simple text saying, "I'm thinking of you, you don't have to answer," can show you care.

**Sad Statistics:**
- One in four pregnancies end in loss. This is an estimate.
- 23 million miscarriages happen globally each year.

In October 2023, which was Pregnancy and Infant Loss Awareness Month, 17,000 individuals visited our website and accessed our information for longer than three minutes.

At Pink Elephants Support Network, we offer phone peer support, live chat, and online communities where people can connect. Each month, over 15,000 participants join these groups. The accessibility of our services means that at any hour, I can open my laptop or phone and get support with an element of anonymity. Over 50 percent of the posts in our online communities are anonymous, which is both beautiful and heartbreaking.

**How can we support you?**
Our main vision is that no one should go through this alone. We want to be there for women, providing support and validation as they navigate their loss. We empathize with their experience, understanding that it is personal to them and that any reaction is okay. We are happy to connect them to organizations like Pink Elephants Support Network so they can seek the support they need.

We gratefully accept donations from those who can contribute, as it empowers us to continue our passionate work for others. More work is needed, and we can do it by raising awareness about this often-taboo topic.

---

**Podcast Episode 422:** Sam Payne - CEO of The Pink Elephants Support Network, May 13, 2024
**Contact Information:** https://www.pinkelephants.org.au/

# Susan Dealis Gobbo

## Beyond the Glamorous Expatriate Story

*"A leader takes people where they want to go.
A great leader takes people where they don't necessarily
want to go, but ought to be."*
- Rosalynn Carter, former First Lady of the United States

Susan and I met in 2005 at Nestlé in the United States, where I oversaw the visa process for the Gobbo family. Now, a few years later, Susan is helping others who come to the US because she has been through that process herself. It always sounds glamorous to move to a foreign country as an expat, but there are many steps to navigate before you get there.

Susan - I think it's important to shed light on the reality of expat life, which often seems glamorous from the outside. I'm from Brazil and came to the United States in 2005 with my family, following my husband who was transferred here by his company. We brought our 5-year-old daughter and embarked on what seemed like an exciting adventure but quickly became a challenging journey, especially for me as the trailing spouse.

While there were many lunches with other expat wives, I often felt very alone in the new country, far from any family support. I would read articles related to my previous job as a physical therapist in English, but I wasn't fluent in the language. In Brazil, I was the head of a department, which was a big part of my identity. In the States, I had nothing. I would drop off my daughter at school and then go to my own classes to learn English. This was before smartphones, so I was constantly worried about what might happen to my daughter while I was in class.

My husband, meanwhile, was at work, continuing his daily routine. His life was easier, while mine was completely turned upside down. When we were invited to parties, I didn't want to go because I felt like I had nothing to share with others. Back in Brazil, I earned my own salary, but now I had to ask for money, even to buy a gift for my husband. This was very awkward and made me feel smaller and smaller.

**Fast forward:**
As a physical therapist, I used to help people recover from injuries and illnesses. Now, I help people flourish in a new culture, touching many lives. Everyone has a gift and calling in life, and mine is to offer help, provide support, and connect people in a new country.

Today, the International Spouses/Expat Women group includes over 890 women from more than ninety-five countries. They join small groups for fun social and cultural gatherings, providing support, friendship, and guidance to international women who move to the St. Louis area.

The group isn't just social; it also has a professional focus. I help these women connect with companies and organizations, find jobs, volunteer opportunities, and secure positions on boards.

In 2017, I co-founded the International Mentoring Program (IMP), which pairs international women with local women and their families to help integrate them into our community. We also welcome Americans moving here from other states, connecting them as mentors to this diverse group of international talents joining our city. Currently, our program includes over six hundred women, evenly split between internationals and Americans, representing sixty-seven different countries.

The IMP is designed to benefit both groups: American women can share their cultural knowledge as mentors, while also gaining insights from interacting with international and local women. Our growth has been substantial, and in 2022, we officially became a 501c3 organization, with me serving as the Program Director.

Participation in our programs is free; members only cover their own expenses for any activities they choose to join. These programs are open to both women employees and partners/spouses looking to connect and engage in our vibrant community.

---

**Podcast Episode 370:** Susan Dealis Gobbo – St. Louis International Spouses / Expat Women, July 3, 2023
**Contact Information:** Www.mentorprogramstl.org

# Hulya Kurt

## **Break free from YOUR Hamster Wheel**

*"Don't compromise yourself. You are all you've got."*
- Janis Joplin, American singer

Hulya Kurt lives by the beautiful Lake Geneva in Switzerland and exudes a contagious, uplifting energy that sets her apart. Her enthusiasm shines through with pride, pizzazz, and always a smile. I first met Hulya at the OWIT International Spring Retreat in Washington, D.C.

Hulya - originally from Turkey but grew up in Germany. At eighteen, my family moved back to Istanbul, where I started my career in the days before internet and PCs, using a typewriter. I began as a sales secretary but was determined to climb the corporate ladder. Along the way, I married and had a son.

I received a job offer in 2005 to relocate with my family to Geneva. After more than ten years in Geneva headquarters, it was obvious that the company would be downsizing, thus I launched my company with a logo and website, ready to offer workshops. I obtained a coaching certification with a focus on career coaching and have since added many disciplines to my toolkit.

**"Break Free from Your Hamster Wheel: Your Travel Itinerary to Professional Fulfillment."**
Feeling stuck in your career? Whether you want to advance, change paths, or start your own business, this book can guide you like a GPS to break free and head in a new direction. It starts with developing the right mindset to take action! Then, it offers practical advice on creating an action plan to move forward...

**What's your secret to success?**

- I'm a doer—I love what I do.
- Give me a task, and I'm in action immediately.
- No overthinking—I just go for it.
- I delegate tasks instead of trying to do everything myself.
- Work smart, not just hard, and always find joy in what I do.

In 2024 and 2025, I'll proudly serve as the international president for OWIT International (owit.org), an organization empowering women in international trade. I'm passionate about my role and fully engaged in its responsibilities.
**How do you create a good routine in the morning?**

In the morning, I stick to a rigorous routine. I start by avoiding my phone—absolutely no checking! Instead, I prepare my special juice: water infused with mint, ginger, and lemon, followed by savoring a cup of coffee. Exercise is a must for me, dedicating 30 minutes daily to yoga, walking, or hiking. This morning ritual prepares me mentally for the busy day ahead.

I ensure to plan downtime in the middle of the day to recharge. Living in Geneva, surrounded by nature, offers me ample opportunities. I take a one-hour luxury break to immerse myself in the lush greenery. I stroll around and indulge in a cappuccino at my favorite café in the neighborhood.

Enjoy your cappuccino!

---

**Podcast Episode 309:** Hulya Kurt - Break Free from your Hamster Wheel, June 20, 2022
**Contact Information:** https://innkick.com/

# Hilary Barry

## The LadyAgri Impact Journey

*"Never underestimate the power of a small group*
*of committed people to change the world.*
*In fact, it is the only thing that ever has."*
— Margaret Mead, American cultural anthropologist

Hilary Barry - who is originally from Ireland, founded and leads **LadyAgri Impact Investment Hub** in Brussels, Belgium. We met in Brussels in 2022 when I spoke about Lipstick Leadership.

**The Birth of LadyAgri:**
LadyAgri Impact Investment Hub, a nonprofit organization, was founded in 2018 by Hilary and her partners after her extensive 27-year career in Africa. The goal is to empower women in agriculture, from farm to table, by providing access to financing, climate-smart equipment, technology, and technical support. These women, often unrecognized but vital to our food systems, play a crucial role in advancing cooperatives, agribusinesses, and small and medium enterprises (SMEs).

The concept for LadyAgri originated in Senegal many years ago when Hilary, a young technical expert, questioned how to ensure that women in agricultural value chains and food systems were acknowledged, valued, and supported. In

2016, Hilary found support from like-minded experts, leading to the formation of the LadyAgri alliance.

By 2018, the launch of LadyAgri marked a significant step forward, aiming to disrupt positively and bring about change in the sector.

Today, LadyAgri operates throughout Africa, playing different roles depending on where they fit within the system—whether as a female entrepreneur, cooperative leader, government official, development partner, donor, private sector entity, investor, or financial provider.

The organization faces realities head-on, much like a child pointing out that "the emperor has no clothes." LadyAgri challenges the disparity between countries with advanced technological capabilities and those where women still lack essential resources like energy, water, land, transportation, equipment, and technology.

LadyAgri believes that achieving gender equality is key to addressing extreme poverty, hunger, malnutrition, and building resilience against climate change. They argue that investing in women makes economic sense.

**Our Community and Impact:**
LadyAgri, a nonprofit association, operates as a cooperative of technical experts with twenty-seven members from seventeen different nationalities. The group is composed of 60% women and 40% men, highlighting its dedication to diversity and inclusion. Their mission is to empower women

and youth, aiming to strengthen communities and countries. LadyAgri mobilizes resources inclusively, breaking down silos and cultural barriers to promote collaborative efforts.

**Success Amidst Challenges:**
When the pandemic struck, LadyAgri was just over a year old. Travel restrictions made it challenging to meet with women-led SMEs, cooperatives, and partners. Despite these obstacles, the support from the women they worked with remained strong. Late-night WhatsApp messages conveyed belief in their mission, urging them to persevere and amplify their voices to decision-makers.

One significant success story involved a woman-led company in Kenya that had to lay off all two hundred employees due to the pandemic. Her existing investors reached out to LadyAgri for assistance. A supportive 'sisterly' approach was needed to guide the woman CEO and her family through the crisis.

With LadyAgri providing careful advice and exploring options, the company decided to revise their business plan, restructure, and diversify their product line. This calculated risk paid off when, within six months, the company was able to rehire their female workforce. By focusing on local and regional markets, the company not only survived but thrived despite the global challenges.

These success stories caught the attention of the King Baudouin Foundation, leading to the creation of the Friends of LadyAgri philanthropic fund in 2021, offering tax exemptions to supporters.

In 2023, the LadyAgri fund financed a climate-smart food processing center benefiting 720 women in Togo. The project, which received over $86,000 in investment, included solar dryers, advanced food processing equipment, storage facilities, and access to finance, supported by tailored technical assistance from the LadyAgri team in Togo.

In recognition of these efforts, LadyAgri received the Best Sustainability Project award from the Belgian Federation of Women CEOs in September 2023.

This accolade underscores the organization's perseverance and commitment to its core mission.

"LadyAgri is committed for the long term… join us in this marathon…because investing in women is smart economics."

---

**Podcast Episode 332:** Hilary Barry - Founder and CEO of LadyAgri, Impact Investment Hub, November 14, 2022
**Contact Information:** https://www.lady-agri.org/

# Dr. Monika V. Kronbügel

## From Consulting to Industries to Politics

*"We cannot just look at a country by looking at charts, graphs, and modelling the economy.
Behind the numbers there are people."*
– Christine Lagarde, President, European Central Bank

Since we last spoke, Monika has become an inspiring political figure, dedicating her time to topics like zero emissions, innovation, and diversity. Thank you for your outstanding work!

Monika - is the CEO and Chief People & Organization Officer (CPOO) of **Global DiVision GmbH**, based in Schleswig-Holstein, near Hamburg, Germany. She is an expert in strategic communication and management, as well as a politician. We initially connected through a mutual friend on Facebook, which always makes for a cool and unbelievable story! I'm grateful for this professional connection that has also turned into a dear friendship.

**A new chapter for your career:**
Monika - I'm entering a new chapter that still aligns with my life's journey. Even before the pandemic, I had decided to move away from my consulting and coaching background. I asked myself, "What do I really want now that I'm in my

mid-fifties? What will I do in the next ten to fifteen years?" Reflecting on this, I realized the importance of paying it forward and giving back. It's not just about personal gain; I want to share my decades of learning with others and contribute to our collective well-being. This led me to pursue a path in politics.

When you aim to influence our societal structures, politics is where decisions are primarily made. Instead of just complaining, I chose to take action to bring about meaningful change.

Monika entered the local elections in May 2023 in Schleswig-Holstein, Germany, where municipal councils are being newly elected. Drawing from my advisory work with various companies, I've observed parallels. It's essential to engage all employees in the change process so that everyone understands and aligns with the organization's future direction.

**Why is this important?**
In reality, most of the actual work is done by those on the ground—the workers and teams in offices—not by management. That's why it's crucial to involve all resources. This perspective applies to politics as well. Often, decisions at the state or federal level are made without truly understanding the real concerns and needs of the people. Communities and municipalities are often overlooked in these discussions. Take digitization, for example—a pressing issue today (or perhaps, are we already behind?). Whether it's improving digital tools in schools or

streamlining administrative processes like IDs, permits, or taxes, decisions are typically imposed from the top down. This approach means that people are expected to comply without their voices being heard.

From my experience in various industries, I've seen this pattern repeated—it's time for a change. This is one of the reasons I've chosen to enter politics now: to ensure that the decisions made reflect the actual needs and desires of the population, by listening to and understanding their daily realities.

**How are you changing that?**
We set up Commuter Café (Pendlerkaffee) stations at local train stations to engage with people during their morning commute—the real individuals we aimed to connect with. Starting at 6 o'clock in the morning, we offered free coffee. While not everyone had time to chat, some enjoyed the coffee and lively conversations, fostering community connections. This initiative conveyed a clear message: I am here for the community.

There's still much more to do, and Dr. Monika V. Kronbügel brings her enthusiasm, passion, and extensive knowledge to serve the people wholeheartedly.

**Fast forward:**
Dr. Monika V. Kronbügel went door-to-door, introducing herself and asking questions like, "What can local politics do for you?" in 2023 and "What are your wishes or hopes for European politics?" in 2024 as she was also a candidate for the European Parliament.

---

**Podcast Episode 360:** Dr. Monika V. Kronbügel – a new Career in Politics (Episode in German), April 29, 2023
**Contact Information:**
https://www.global-division.com/en/home.html
https://kronbuegel.eu/

# Val Quinn

## Create YOUR Best LIFE

*"If there is one thing I've learned in life,
it's the power of using your voice."*
– Michelle Obama, former First Lady of the United States

Val and I met at the Vital Voices Conference in Washington, DC. She is an ambassador and mentor for the Vital Voices Global Partnership, a non-profit organization dedicated to advancing women's leadership worldwide. Val spoke passionately about reimagining life after job change or loss—a topic that deeply resonated with me.

Val Quinn is an executive, life coach, and business trainer, and she previously served as the managing director of The Coca-Cola Company. She's also an Ironman. Her passion project involved curating a book featuring over forty stories contributed pro-bono by various authors. Each writer shared their personal stories, and all net proceeds from the anthology go to charity.

Val's goal is to raise €53k, the cost to fund a guide dog for life being allocated to a visually impaired person, including training, vet fees, and food. (The €53k is the actual cost for the full life of a dog from pup to old age/death) This initiative aims to change lives for the better through all the net proceeds from her book.

**Why this book?**
The inspiration for the book came when I left Coca-Cola with a voluntary redundancy package. At the same time, I had lost sight in my right eye. I visited the eye doctor, who told me, "We've restored your eyesight for now. Science is wonderful, but you have an issue with your retina in both eyes, and you will need future operations. There's a small chance you might go blind."

It was a shocking revelation, to say the least. I thought, "Maybe this is the universe giving me a sign." Perhaps it was time to consider doing something else. This experience motivated me to accept the voluntary redundancy package. Suddenly finding myself retired at the age of fifty-three was unexpected, and I found myself at home wondering what to do next—it all happened quite quickly.

I started reflecting on my own journey. I realized there are many people with similar experiences. It struck me that sharing my career path and the decisions I've made—living in London, the States, and Ireland, working in sales, marketing, and general management, and completing an Ironman triathlon—could be insightful. After training in coaching and mentoring, I felt compelled to share my learnings with others for inspiration.

Instead of just telling my own story, I believed it would be more impactful to hear from others. Many might have started out loving their jobs but now feel stuck. Long-term stagnation can affect mental health, and they may want to change but don't know how.

My goal was to encourage people to share their authentic stories to help and inspire others. I also recognized that the challenges I face as an Irish person living in Ireland may differ from those faced by people elsewhere in the world. I take pride in having a diverse network to draw upon.

The book features stories from both men and women, offering a wide range of backgrounds:

- An actress from Los Angeles who has made significant life changes.
- An international rugby player from Ireland who transitioned into the business world after retiring from professional sports.
- A radio DJ from New York who is also a triathlete with severe visual impairment, focusing on motivational speaking to inspire others.
- Susanne's journey from Switzerland to New York, losing a job in the corporate world (the American dream!) and forging her own path.

My aim is to inspire and motivate others to take that next big step, not just through my own story but through a variety of stories that can hopefully inspire others as well.

---

**Podcast Episode 376**: Val Quinn - Reimagining, Rewiring or Retiring, August 12, 2023
**Contact Information:** https://www.tilly.ie/
Buy the book and support her cause:
https://www.amazon.com/Create-Your-Best-Life-Stories/dp/0994210558

# Sarah Gabriel-Régis

## Fulfilling her Childhood Dream

*"Nothing in life is to be feared, it is only to be understood.*
*Now is the time to understand more,*
*so that we may fear less."*
– Marie Curie, first women to be awarded a Nobel Prize


Sarah - a French Caribbean who grew up in Guadeloupe and now lives in Brussels, Belgium. I am a biologist, regulatory affairs manager, entrepreneur, runner, aikidoka, coffee enthusiast, and mother. In my career, I lived in Germany, where I completed my PhD. There, I learned to be structured by the Germans.

Coming from the Caribbean and French Latin culture, I wasn't used to the German discipline and structure in their daily lives. We both met in Brussels when I gave a talk about Lipstick Leadership a few years ago.

**What are your dreams for the near future?**
I want to start a coffee plantation in Guadeloupe, fulfilling a dream I've had for the past 20 years—now it's becoming a reality. My family owned a small plantation with a house and land where, as a child, I helped my grandparents collect coffee beans by removing the cherries and drying them. It was a fun and peaceful experience, and that's exactly what I aim to recreate.

178

Starting this project requires immense patience because after planting coffee, it takes at least two years before the first beans can be harvested, and about five years for a full production cycle. My vision includes not just coffee but creating a whole ecosystem blending agricultural and ecological elements.

In addition to coffee, I plan to cultivate cacao, which helps maintain the coffee trees by preventing excessive weed growth. I also intend to grow vanilla, as it thrives in this environment and provides shade beneficial for coffee plants. My goal is to establish a harmonious coexistence where coffee and other crops complement each other, fostering a sustainable and thriving agricultural venture.

These days, I travel frequently to Guadeloupe to build connections. Sadly, I no longer have land or family there since my parents passed away. However, I have forged friendships and am reconnecting with people in the community.

In Guadeloupe, more than anywhere else, networking plays a crucial role—a lesson I learned at Harvard University in the United States. Harvard taught me the art of networking, which is highly valued in the U.S. culture. In Germany, I learned discipline, but networking wasn't emphasized as much.

I excel at connecting with others, sharing my current endeavors, and building relationships. I understand that relationships are paramount in starting a business. It's essential to have the right people in key roles. Often, hiring talented individuals doesn't guarantee they'll be the right fit for the team. This realization is pivotal for my business venture.

I'm not inventing anything new; I'm drawing from ancestral practices that have been used for generations. However, I aim to enhance these methods with modern knowledge and technology. Combining the best of both worlds—traditional wisdom with contemporary advancements—is my approach.

Today, people are more mindful about their purchases, prioritizing transparency and ethical sourcing.

My business will be fair-trade certified and women-owned, reflecting these values. Originally, I planned to sell green coffee beans exclusively.

However, I realized that to sell quality beans, testing and roasting are essential. Therefore, I've expanded my project to include the entire process—from farming to the cup. This means I will also handle roasting and offer barista services.

**Visualization:**
When I was a child, Guadeloupe was primarily a tourist destination for people from France. Now, it has evolved into an international vacation hotspot. Modern travelers seek more than just beach relaxation—they crave unique experiences and exploration. Visiting my coffee plantation, savoring local coffee, and discussing the ecosystem and

coffee culture will be a hidden gem. It's an invitation to enjoy something special and authentic.

Bonne chance! Let's share a cup of coffee soon at my plantation.

---

**Podcast Episode 345:** Sarah Gabriel-Régis – Coffee in Guadalupe, February 6, 2023
**Contact Information:** website coming soon!

# Diana Nash

## Unveiling a Taboo: Death and Dying

*"If we could see that everything, even tragedy,
is a gift in disguise,
we would then find the best way to nourish the soul."*
– Elisabeth Kuebler-Ross, Swiss-American psychiatrist,
author, pioneer in near-death studies

Diana was my academic counselor at Marymount Manhattan College in New York when I decided to return to college a few years ago. Initially aiming for a Bachelor's Degree in Speech Pathology, I found it wasn't available part-time, so I chose psychology instead—a decision I've never regretted. Marymount Manhattan College holds a special place in my heart, where many lasting friendships began through mutual support and camaraderie. It truly feels like a magical place.

Diana - brings over 20 years of experience as a grief therapist and adjunct professor of psychology at Marymount Manhattan College. She holds a Master's Degree in Counseling Psychology from New York University. In addition to teaching courses on death, bereavement, and psychology, Diana runs a private practice. Here, she supports clients facing grief, depression, anxiety, and various life challenges with compassion and expertise.

182

**How did you get into this?** Like many therapists, I was drawn to my specialization for personal reasons. At the time, I experienced the loss of two family members, followed shortly by the passing of a third person. I sought bereavement counseling to help me navigate this grief journey personally, and it sparked a deep passion within me.

**Death and dying:** Certainly, death is an integral part of life; it's as much about life as it is about death. In Western culture, we often avoid discussing death until we attend a funeral or memorial service. People are reluctant to open up about the deep grief and pain they feel. Unlike physical injuries like a broken arm, which are visible with a cast, grieving is an internal, invisible experience. This internal, psychic pain makes the grieving process particularly challenging.

**What is the right thing to say?** Others may not realize you're grieving, and even if they do, they might struggle with how to react. There's often a fear of saying the wrong thing, which can lead to hesitation or avoiding the topic altogether. Some people even worry that grief is contagious or fear being too close to someone who is grieving.

It's common for people to admit, "I don't know what to say." Sometimes, the best response is simply acknowledging that uncertainty: "I don't know the right words, but I'm here beside you. I care for you, I love you, and I'm here to support you."

During these moments, our presence is incredibly powerful. Just being there, offering support, love, and genuine compassion, can mean the world to someone who is grieving. It's important to recognize that everyone experiences grief differently, and showing empathy in a sincere and authentic manner can make a significant difference.

**The work as a grief therapist:** Diana often faces questions about how long the grieving process will take and whether someone is handling it correctly. She emphasizes that there's no right or wrong way to grieve—it's a personal journey. The duration of grief can vary based on circumstances, such as the sudden loss of a young, healthy individual versus the passing of an elderly person with a long-term illness. In her practice, Diana typically works with clients for about six months, often starting with weekly sessions and gradually spacing them out as progress is made—from weekly to bi-weekly, then monthly.

In social settings, when Diana mentions her work as a grief counselor, reactions vary widely. Some people may shy away or change the subject, while others are drawn to share their own grief experiences. She believes that discussing grief openly and processing it with trusted individuals—whether friends, family, clergy, or therapists—is essential for healing and nurturing the soul.

---

**Podcast Episode 399:** Diana Nash - the Grief Therapist, January 8, 2024
**Contact Information:**
www.psychologytoday.com / https://www.betterhelp.com/

# Shona McDonald

## The Right Type of Wheelchair to Communicate

*"They'll tell you you're too loud – that you need to wait your turn and ask the right people for permission. Do it anyway."*
- Alexandria Ocasio-Cortez, American politician, and activist

Shona is the founder of **ShonaquipSE**, a social enterprise in South Africa. Despite being dyslexic and discouraged by her parents from attending university, she pursued her passion for art and sculpting instead. We met online at a networking event with OWIT.

In my view, Shona is not just a businesswoman and visionary, but also a dedicated mother who passionately demonstrates what is achievable to the world.

Shona - when my second daughter was born with severe disabilities, I faced medical advice suggesting institutionalization and having another child instead. This sparked my determination to prove them wrong. I began by focusing on meeting her basic needs, like feeding and communication, as she struggled with these from an early age and couldn't communicate verbally. Starting with a small NGO called INTERFACE, I aimed to teach alternative methods of communication, not just for my daughter but for others facing similar challenges. This initiative grew into a national organization training therapists and parents in Augmentative and Alternative Communication (AAC). Through this journey, I realized that physical independence is crucial for effective communication—without it, people are often overlooked and not taken seriously.

Designing and building an electric wheelchair transformed my daughter's life. It enabled her to move independently, and move around freely. We understood how to help her if she wanted a drink, she'd drive to the fridge, if she wanted to go outside, she'd drive to the door. The wheelchair became more than mobility—it became a tool for her to express herself. With time, we also taught her to read, paving the way for her inclusion in mainstream education, making her one of the first children in South Africa to achieve this. This experience taught me firsthand the profound impact that the right wheelchair can have. It's not just about mobility; it's about fostering independence, inclusion, happiness, and overall physical well-being. Conversely, the wrong wheelchair can lead to serious health issues and worsened disabilities, potentially even shortening life expectancy.

Our journey expanded as we collaborated with government and therapists to ensure that suitable equipment, tailored for both rugged terrain and individual needs, became accessible through South Africa's healthcare system, especially for those unable to afford it. Starting in our garage and home, we soon moved into a small factory, and within a few years, expanded to a larger facility to accommodate our growth.

We also developed training courses for therapists and doctors. This effort caught the attention of the World Health Organization, (WHO) which recognized me as an expert in wheelchair provision for Southern Africa and invited me to contribute to the World Health Wheelchair Guidelines. These guidelines emphasize that providing a wheelchair is just one part of a broader support system necessary for families and individuals with disabilities.

Our initiatives now extend beyond wheelchair provision and healthcare training to include outreach clinics and advocacy. The profits generated support efforts to change societal attitudes toward disability and influence policy implementation. Through community dialogues, we foster understanding of disability and promote inclusion in workplaces and schools, aiming to create environments where all individuals can thrive.

**Shorten the Queue:** We initiated a wheelchair fund to support children who do not qualify for government assistance. Our goal is to alleviate the lengthy wait times and waiting lists these children face to receive their wheelchairs. In some cases, children endure up to six years of waiting, leading to severe pain and deformities during that time. Our passion lies in **shortening the queue** and ensuring children receive the right device that addresses their specific needs effectively.

---

**Podcast Episode 421:** Shona McDonald – Founder of ShonaquipSE – Shorten the Queue, May 6, 2024
**Contact Information:** https://shonaquipse.org.za/.

# LIME-LIGHT

*"One honest voice is louder than a crowd."*
– Reese Witherspoon, actress

No one achieves anything alone, and I owe more thanks than I can express to the countless individuals who have supported me along the way.

I am grateful to Destiny J. Cool for creating numerous creative and wonderful posts on social media. Additionally, I extend my thanks to Mimi Ugweje for meticulously fact-checking the book with great attention to detail and providing valuable quotes.

There were many wonderful secret collaborators who helped make this dream come true for me, again and again. Finally, thanks to the many readers who reviewed all these pages when the book was still a very rough, raw draft. I appreciate the honest feedback and guidance you provided, which helped improve its flow. Thank you for making it happen.

Thanks for being with me on this journey. If you enjoy the book, please consider sharing it with someone who might also appreciate it.

# LIFE OF THE AUTHOR



Susanne Mueller, M.A., is from Switzerland and currently lives in New York City. She holds a Master's Degree in Organizational Development & Leadership from Columbia University, and a Bachelor's Degree in Psychology from Marymount Manhattan College. Additionally, Susanne is certified in Executive Coaching from Columbia University. She is the CEO and Founder of Susanne Mueller Consulting in New York City, coaching business executives across over 60 countries. She is also a TEDx Speaker "Running and Life: 5K Formula for your success."

Beyond her professional achievements, Susanne has completed 1 Ironman Triathlon in Lake Placid, participated in 26 marathon races, and successfully summited Mt. Kilimanjaro.

Susanne Mueller, M.A., is a multifaceted professional who engages as a weekly blogger and podcaster, sharing insights on leadership and personal development. She is also a published author, known for her books "Take it from the Ironwomen: Global Business Coaching with Sports Parallels" (2017) and "Lipstick Leadership" (2021). Her writings blend her expertise in business coaching with lessons drawn from the world of sports, offering actionable strategies for success.

# LECTURE WITH THE AUTHOR

### How does a Typical Day look like for You?

*"We learn from very young people, and they learn from us, too. That's the way it's always been."*
— Camilla Parker Bowles, Queen of the United Kingdom

**Destiny:** Can you give us an idea of what a typical day looks like for you as an entrepreneur and executive coach?

**Susanne:** Well, the first thing I do is check my phone, even though they say you shouldn't! But when you work globally, and you have a 7 AM meeting, you need to make sure everyone's on the same page. I double-check my calendar to avoid missing any appointments. Although, I have to admit, there's really no such thing as a typical day. We need to stay flexible and adaptable, always ready to go with the flow. Being proactive and anticipating what could happen next is key in this dynamic environment.

**Destiny:** What roles and experiences have shaped your journey as a solo entrepreneur?

**Susanne:** With a Bachelor's Degree in Psychology and a Master's in Organizational Development and Leadership from Columbia University, my career began in sales and marketing within the airline industry. I found joy in project work and leveraging my background in psychology. Today, I blend these insights with coaching, focusing on leadership development and skill enhancement for business leaders.

**Destiny:** What do you find most fulfilling about your work, and what challenges do you encounter?

**Susanne:** The greatest satisfaction comes from seeing my clients succeed after coaching them. It's incredibly rewarding when they get promoted or share how much better they feel thanks to our coaching sessions.

On the flip side, one of the more frustrating aspects of being a solo entrepreneur is when clients cancel last minute. In those moments, I either turn to other tasks I can work on or take a well-deserved break with a cup of coffee.

**Destiny**: What skills do you consider essential for your work?

**Susanne:** Listening attentively, asking insightful questions, and maintaining a non-judgmental approach are crucial. As an executive coach, the focus is always on the individual sharing their story. It's about guiding them with questions like, "What insights can we gain from your experience?" and "What are the key takeaways for you?"

**Destiny:** What skills do you find most crucial for your work?

**Susanne:** The most important skills are active listening, asking insightful questions, and maintaining a non-judgmental approach. As an executive coach, my focus is entirely on the person sharing their story. It involves asking the right questions to delve deeper.

**Destiny:** How did you develop and apply these skills?
**Susanne**: I've honed these skills through years of coaching experience and by learning from other coaches. I approach coaching like a journalist crafting an engaging story, always striving to ask the right questions and bring out meaningful insights.

**Destiny:** What advice do you have for others when it comes to networking?
**Susanne:** Networking is about building and nurturing genuine connections. It's hard work—look closely at the word "networking," it spells out "working."

**Destiny:** What advice would you give to young people aspiring to be entrepreneurs?
**Susanne:** Dive in and give it a try—don't wait. But be prepared for reality: it's demanding, relentless work. Entrepreneurship is a 24/7 commitment without a clear endpoint.

---

**Podcast Episode 300:** Destiny J. Cool – Interview with Susanne - How does a typical day look like? April 18, 2022
**Contact Information:** www.susannemueller.biz